FOURTH

Freya Aquarone graduated from the University of Cambridge in 2016 with a degree in sociology, and has spent the past year working in academic research and volunteering in a school for excluded teenagers (alongside accidentally becoming a Liberal Democrat activist). Freya's main interest is alternative education; she attended the controversial democratic school Summerhill for two years and was taught at home for most of her teens. Freya lives in rural Norfolk, where she spends a good deal of time running through fields of wheat.

Steffan Aquarone is a UK digital entrepreneur and speaker whose experiences range from film to payments. He has consulted and trained for big brands and spoken around the world on innovation, entrepreneurship and digital marketing. In 2014, he was voted by university and secondary school students as one of the most influential new media figures under the age of 30. Steff lives in Norfolk with his wife and son. He is Freya's brother.

Fourth to First

How to win a local election in under six months

Freya Aquarone
Steffan Aquarone

THE REAL PRESS
www.therealpress.co.uk

Published in 2017 by the Real Press.
www.therealpress.co.uk
© Freya Aquarone and Steffan Aquarone

ISBN (print) 978-1912119653
ISBN (ebooks) 978-1912119646

For Jill and Felix

Contents

We have tried to make this a truthful and authentic account of our experiences, without upsetting anyone. In fact, we used the best of our abilities to record facts accurately, and anonymise people where necessary. Please accept our sincere apologies if you're upset or offended by anything that happened.

1
Melton Constable: getting to WIN!
(*Steff*)

I can't actually remember when it was I decided to stand, or exactly what prompted me. In the absence of fact, I will blame Ed Maxfield, North Norfolk Lib Dem organiser and Parliamentary office manager to Norman Lamb, North Norfolk's MP.

Gmail has been a fantastic tool in writing this book because it is so good for searching correspondence. All I can find from the early days of the campaign, however, is an email from Ed on 5 September 2016 saying: "Some thoughts on Melton Constable county division". That is why I am blaming him for getting all this started.

This is what it said:

MELTON CONSTABLE: getting to WIN![1]

---

[1] This is the sort of awful use of capitalisation and

The result in 2013 was:

Turnout: 3205 (42.65%) – the fourth highest in the whole of Norfolk

David Ramsbotham	UKIP	1144	36%
Russell Wright	Conservative	945	29%
Callum Ringer	Labour	568	18%
Jacqueline Howe	Lib Dem	355	11%
Thomas Robinson	Green	193	6%

We ran a paper candidate in 2013, so the result understates our potential. In 2009, the result was Conservative 1,415; Lib Dem 1,015; UKIP 532; Green 317; Labour 182. The last time we contested the wards strongly was in the 2007 district elections when the votes cast across the four wards was: Lib Dem 1,870; Conservative 1,755; Others 209.

---

rhetoric that appears to have dominated the party's local literature for decades. "Literature" in politics-speak, is a generous word: usually all it has in common with literature is that it's printed on paper.

"Propaganda" is the word I preferred to use when I bumped into the people I was delivering it to, inevitably while they were trying to get into their houses, or pacify their (ridiculous) dogs.

The division

On the current count, the division is made up of:
7,526 People
3,980 Doors

We have phone numbers for 1,478 households. We have email addresses for 197 people.

Supporters

There are 17 members in the division. The list of 'supporters' (members, donors, past deliverers and poster sites) runs to 134 people in 121 households. These are the hot prospects for an early call to sign up to help, join or have posters.

The target pool of voters

The winning post to aim for is 1,200 votes. Creating a list made up of supporters and squeeze voters then removing those who never vote and those in the very smallest villages generates a list of 1,300 *households* (about 1/3 of the division and comfortably enough to win). These are the people to concentrate on with canvassing and direct mail. They are split between villages in the following numbers:

Polling District	Doors
UG1 - Briston	444

UR1 - Hindolveston	108
UY1 - Great Ryburgh	101
KU4 - Corpusty	96
UW1 - Melton Const.	95
KN1 - Bodham	89
UL1 - Fulmodeston	83
VC4 - Little Snoring	80
KY4 - Edgefield	63
VD4 - Stibbard	45
KF4 - Baconsthorpe	39
VE4 - Swanton Novers	35
VN4 - Wood Norton	22

Issues

As we found in Astley, the demographic profile of the division will be slightly younger and slightly better off than the North Norfolk average so health and care will be less of an issue. The division also has no coastline, so issues relating to erosion etc will not apply.

It is such a geographic spread that Fakenham, Holt, Sheringham and Aylsham will all be focal points for different villages. Digital connectivity will be a significant issue. Speeding through villages will be too. The Bodham wind turbine was a major in the past (and opposition to it probably won David R the election in 2013), but this has gone quiet recently.

Opponents

The incumbent will not be easy to beat as he is an established figure in the area but the Astley by-election result shows that he is beatable. He may also not stand for re-election. Russell Wright will not be standing again.

Communications plan

[the bit we need to develop but it needs to start with a residents' survey!]

Ed M
5/9/16

So that was that: we came fourth last time. But ten years ago in a district election, we had enough combined votes in the area to win a county seat. Still: that was before the coalition, before tuition fees, when people in North Norfolk knew very little about the Liberal Democrats and probably assumed Norman Lamb was the only member...

Ed's missive revealed to me something that, looking back, makes complete sense but which the uninitiated won't have a clue about until someone points it out to them: winning elections is a numbers game.

It's a numbers game

"Of course it's a numbers game," I hear you cry. "It's about the number of people who vote for you". Yes – but before that, it's a numbers game too. And it's all down to how you focus and prioritise.

"The winning pool to aim for is 1,200 votes". That means, based on the last election's winning candidate getting 1,144 votes, we should expect to win if we can get 1,200 people to vote for us.[2] And from this comes the indefatigable logic of local elections: **getting your supporters out to vote makes a bigger difference than persuading people to change their minds.**

Here's why. We knew that more than 350 people would probably turn up and vote Liberal Democrat without being asked to.[3] This meant

---

[2] As it happens, turnout was higher than normal, as both I and Annie Claussen-Reynolds, my Tory opponent, fought active campaigns, and she came second with over 1,200 votes. Plus the collapse of UKIP nationally re-concentrated voters around two choices, which was more obvious in the 2009 county and 2007 district election results.

[3] We know this because of a recent election where we

focusing on how to find the other 850 people to get to 1,200.

In the previous election, 2850 people had voted something other than Lib Dem. But that left 3,205 people who didn't show up. The logic was simple: it was going to be much easier to go and find 850 out of that 3,205 who might be sympathetic to me or the party's policies and persuade them to turn up on the day, than it would to try and convince 850 of the 2,850 who turned up and voted differently last time to change their allegiance and vote for me.

So the focus of our canvassing – by far the biggest part of the campaign – was to go out and find people who might vote Liberal Democrat, and target the campaign at cementing that idea and getting them to turn out on the day. Some of them we had identified in previous campaigns; the rest we would need to go out and find – the elusive 'no data' people.

---

fielded a 'paper candidate'. A paper candidate is not a candidate made out of paper: it's a candidate in name only, who simply appears on the ballot paper. The nice people who do this (with the terrifying risk that they might win by accident, of course) help work out what the 'baseline' support is.

There is a lot more about this later in the book.

Of course, we have no idea how people vote: only what they have told us about their political allegiance in the past, and which elections they have voted in (the 'marked register'). But the big simple idea was: fight a campaign aimed at finding and getting out natural-ish supporters, rather than trying to convince every last voter that they should elect me.

2
How it all started
(Freya)

As a former employee of Norman Lamb MP and the little sister of a county councillor, I am probably – like it or not – shackled to the Liberal Democrats for the rest of my life. It is an unexpected state of affairs for someone who has cancelled their membership three times.

But then, I keep crawling back. The truth is, there is something oddly mystical and alluring about Liberal Democrats, especially in the context of local election battles, and even more so in the rural heartland of North Norfolk. The intense camaraderie in the face of threat, combined with bizarre, Fawlty-Towers-esque adventures in the middle of nowhere, makes for a dream-like experience.

Indeed, looking back over the campaign I am overwhelmed by nostalgia as memories of unsolicited home-made cake, dead ducks hanging from door handles, angry dogs, and helicopters casually parked on front lawns come flooding in.

Every provincial region has its quirks, but

Norfolk is surely the kind of place that dried-up novel writers come to steal the identities of larger-than-life characters.

For somebody who intended to take a year off after university in order to work from home three days a week at a gentle pace, and do a bit of volunteering, running a full-blown election campaign hadn't been high up on my to-do list. But, much as he can wind me up (like every sibling in existence), I would go to the ends of the earth for my big brother.

So when Steff said to me last autumn, *I'm thinking of running for the county council next May*, and asked me whether I would be his campaign manager, I immediately said yes.

Flattered as I was that Steff had asked me to do this, I was also more than a little concerned that my political campaign experience was not exactly wide-reaching. I had worked for Norman Lamb MP back in 2013 as a parliamentary caseworker, and during that time I got involved in a by-election as well as that year's county council elections. But in neither case was I doing any 'managing'.

I was more like a central dogsbody, leafleting and door-knocking whenever and wherever I was told to - and providing some moral support. None of the strategic decisions rested on my shoulders, and there were no volunteer co-ordination, correspondence or crisis-management issues to contend with; all that was done by central office.

On reflection, I think my innocence helped blind me to the enormity of the task. I certainly felt pretty jolly about the whole thing until I looked at the statistics for the area we were supposed to try and win. And by that time it was too late to back out.

As Steff has said, we came fourth in 2013. Even more disheartening was the fact that UKIP had somehow managed to field a competent local councillor, who was our incumbent.

And then there was the area itself: fifteen miles across and not a single town in sight. Melton Constable division is collection of villages, some of which are so sparsely populated that the designation is really pushing descriptive accuracy. There are worryingly few amenities – we once had to drive for 25 minutes to find a letterbox. On the flipside, a lack of public toilets is a great way to make friends.

Once you've got your mental map of loo-stops among the homes of friendly voters, you know you're well on the way to being an accepted member of the community.

Even more ridiculously: despite having been born in Norfolk and having lived there pretty much my whole life, Steff's division was in a part of the county I had literally never been to.

Place names that I'd only ever heard mentioned in passing, as elusive and strange to me as the Outlands in *The Lion King*, suddenly loomed large: *Little Snoring, Melton Constable, Great Ryburgh*.[4] I felt supremely ill-suited for this campaign; as a resident of Blickling, ten miles down the road, I was practically a foreigner in a region that voted overwhelmingly for Brexit.

Add to that a weird surname like 'Aquarone', and the fact that neither Steff nor I had any idea what we were doing, and our chances of success began to look not so much naively optimistic as completely mad.

But for some reason we decided to go ahead with it all. So, just as I had escaped yearly examinations with their routine destruction of the month of May, up went the wall posters. Though this time, rather than quotes and dates, it was A4 print-outs from Google Maps sellotaped together with obscure villages circled in Sharpie, and late spring once again acquired that familiar sense of

---

4 Near the legendary Pudding Norton, which itself - disappointingly – turned out to be just outside the boundaries of the division.

foreboding. Thankfully, it paid off!

The fraught, brilliant and exhausting six months that made up the campaign were some of the most educational and exciting of my life. Truly, there is nothing like an election campaign for dramatically heightening your emotional responses. We were investing so much in a game where there are no prizes for second place. I really can imagine that, had we lost, I would have walked away with a rather bitter view of humanity. Maybe I would have moved to Ipswich just to spite the Norfolk electorate.

Luckily, it turned out alright. And even though the campaign trail introduces you to the best and the worst of human kind, I honestly walked away from polling day – before we even knew the outcome – feeling more hopeful about the state of politics than I have perhaps ever felt in my life.

I will never forget the kindness and the trust shown in my brother by the people of Melton Constable division, even by those who were incensed by his hair.[5] Or his taste in films.[6]

---

[5] One voter was so opposed to Steff's lengthy hair that Steff ended up promising to cut it if he won.

[6] A voter sent Steff an email asking him which five films he would save in the case of a nuclear apocalypse and

But most of all, I will never forget the trust invested in me by Steff, who – for some astonishing reason – decided to allow himself to be ordered around by his little sister for six months.

wasn't at all impressed with the answer!

3
The first campaign
(Steff)

The events in this chapter started on 13 November 2016 and finished on 24 January 2017, just as things were starting to get into gear.

In a way, it was the most important event in the whole campaign. One of my beliefs is that you should live out your values: rather than just talking about them, go out and make something happen that demonstrates them.

I also believe that this is what's missing from a lot of political discourse: there are parliamentarians like Norman who get re-elected even, as he did this year, in the face of a vicious Tory target seat campaign, precisely because of what they have actually done for the past 16 years. But they are rare: most politicians get elected (and rejected) on what they say they will do. And, actually, neither of these things (track record, or promises) is sufficient for explaining the reasons behind your actions: in other words, your political values.

For me, the opportunity was clear: the village

from which the division gets its name, despite being one of the smaller settlements, was about to lose its lollipop lady in the county council's latest round of cuts. Even though all 38 lollipop ladies under threat cost only £150,000 a year in total.

It all started with a tweet – a member of the local community sent a message to Norman Lamb asking him to sign an online petition against the planned withdrawal of the service. He did, and alerted me to it. This was back in November when I had only just decided to become a candidate and I didn't really have a plan. Yet it quickly became clear that this was an issue a lot of people felt very strongly about and I felt I had something to offer.

I also realised it would be an opportunity to explain why I, as a liberal, believe strongly in communities as the ideal unit of organisation in societies, and that it is the role of politicians representing those communities to do things *with* people, not to them or even for them.

First, I got in touch with the person who tweeted, who direct messaged me their phone number. I spoke to her a few days after signing the petition myself, and she put me in touch with the person who was co-ordinating the campaign, a local parent called Karen.

Karen is someone for whom I have developed a huge amount of respect: she is every bit the sort of smart, community-minded person who would belong in the party. I'm not sure how aware she is that I'm working on her to stand as a candidate at some point: she would make a great job of it. But I also think our party is not in a fit state locally to make this a sufficiently attractive offer to people, which explains why we have not always had the best candidates or won as many seats as we should have done.

Karen and a team of parents had got to the stage of co-ordinating a petition that was building momentum, putting up home-made street signs around the village and calling for a public meeting to gauge local opinion. I agreed with her that she would leaflet the local village where the majority of the crossing users lived, and that I would contact the neighbouring village of Briston in the ward where the school itself sat.

Not having any experience of party print and production, but being lucky enough to own an industrial laser printer, I mailmerged a thousand letters and distributed them to the village, inviting them to the community meeting.

On 12 December, in the rainy winter weather, more than fifty people came, including the lollipop lady herself. I was sat on the small panel at the front, which was well chaired by the local parish council chair, at Karen's invitation. My

Liberal Democrat district council colleague also came, as did the Tory council candidate. Needless to say, the council failed to send anyone, but the incumbent UKIP county councillor was in attendance.

He was, it must be said, dutiful in doing some preliminary research into how the decision had been reached. He said it was on the basis of some national guidelines, and that it was very unlikely we would be able to question them. We didn't stand much chance, he said.

I could not believe what I was hearing. How defeatist, I thought! So I stood up and explained that I was interested in helping; that I understood it would probably be an uphill battle, and that the best chance lay in being able to address the decision the council was making on their own terms.

I offered to take on the task of trying to research the guidelines more fully, and gather evidence that would help us challenge the proposed decision. I said if we put the effort into a thoroughly researched, well-informed, sympathetic but adamant case, then we would stand a chance of succeeding.

I did not really get a sense of how people first reacted to this suggestion. There were a lot more contributions from people in attendance, talking about how worried they were, or mentioning near-miss experiences. I jotted these down as I thought they might be useful.

It was not until I exchanged emails with Karen afterwards and started to look at the scale of the task that I realised what I had let myself in for. The guidelines used by local authorities to assess school crossing patrols ran to more than 80 pages. And getting a copy of the report itself cost a whopping £80.

Throughout Christmas, whilst we were away on our first family holiday with our new baby, I worked on the contents of a letter that would become our submission to the council's consultation. I have just found an email from Karen on Christmas Eve talking about one of the more technical points in a section of the letter, which we co-wrote using Google Docs, called "Limitations of the PV^2 formula in relation to child safety and correctness of its application".

Suffice to say, I think a core skill of a politician is being able to understand incredibly niche issues in a very short space of time, and being able to act on them as if you had spent the past ten years specialising in the subject (God help whoever actually has, in this case!). It has happened again more recently when I have had to get to grips with the latest available technology for hauling wind-generated electricity back onshore.

The eventual letter ran to more than ten typed pages and read more like a legal lawsuit than a letter. I don't know how much difference it actually made to the decision, but I think it gave Karen and I, and the other people involved in the campaign, confidence that we were right – not only morally (the crossing patrol was first introduced in the village following a tragic death).[7] But also technically, by the council's own adopted guidelines.

The council had, we believed, miscounted the

---

[7] The victim was six-year-old girl named Natasha Parks and she died on 16 March 1977. I uncovered this remarkably specific fact when I was out in the village knocking on people's doors to see if they'd had a chance to fill in a survey we'd produced, to learn of any 'near misses'. The lady who remembered it recited the tragic details like she'd just read them in a newspaper. More recently, the same lady was able to remember the year that the parish council lobbied to have traffic waiting restrictions put on one of the roads, so I was able to go to the Council Archives and retrieve the relevant minutes. Local knowledge is so valuable, and failing to capture it risks losing so much more than interesting stories.

traffic as well as the children and failed to apply the weightings for all the various additional factors like visibility, footpaths and road junctions.

What happened next was a fantastically fortuitous and entirely accidental masterclass in campaigning.

Dozens of people contributed to the letter, not just me and Karen. A local gentleman did his own traffic counts, which contradicted what the council had captured. People sent in accounts and pictures and descriptions of how they felt about the road, and added all manner of historical and circumstantial context that the assessors had simply failed to take into account.

By the time it was all submitted before the consultation deadline of 8 January, 538 people had signed the petition, making it the most signed petition of all 38 of the sites under threat.

A great many people also put their name to the letter: people from various political parties, including people who were taking a real risk by showing their public support of a campaign against the decisions of their ultimate employer.

We saw the paper that a council officer had produced, which explained why they should withdraw the crossings. Several of the paragraphs from our letter had made it into the report as examples of the responses they had received. And the report, interestingly, did not make a recommendation as we had expected it to: it laid out the case for and against, which I believe is unusual for officer reports.

Then something remarkable happened: the children in the village all made signs. They started to appear around the village, on lampposts and fences. Then an A-board started appearing at the crossing site every morning and afternoon. It said: "Save Our Lollipop Lady".

By this point, the Children's Services Committee at the council had announced the 24 January as the date of their decision. I'd begun speaking to other Liberal Democrat councillors, in particular Brian Hannah, who has since retired from the county council but was one of the members of the committee, and our erstwhile group leader Marie Strong who has been a mentor to me on the council. Brian suggested that we should contact the chair of the committee, and see whether he would accept a copy of our submission in person on the date of the committee meeting.

This was enough to get my imagination going: what if we actually turned up, lots of us, in person, and protested outside County Hall? I didn't know if this was something that happened often or not, but I guessed it was probably our right, and didn't ask anyone who might have told me otherwise.

And so it was that shortly before 7:30 on the morning of the committee meeting, in the freezing cold and fog, I found myself, dressed as a lollipop lady with home-made Stop signs, standing at the top of the steps of County Hall.

And the plan started to work. Karen had sent a press release out a few days before and we'd started to get some attention. The *Eastern Daily Press* published an article on the morning of the committee meeting which included a photo we had taken the day before, at the crossing, with all the children dressed up in their protest gear. I had also received a call from another teacher all the way over in Heacham, who was planning to bring a busload of children over.

Speaking to this teacher made me really glad there were still people in the world who had not been brow-beaten by the national curriculum.[8]

---

[8] One of the things she'd asked me is whether I thought anyone else would be coming with children and I had to say I wasn't sure, as the school in question on my patch had decided it couldn't sanction taking children out of lessons. But I made it clear that I totally agreed with her that it was an absolutely brilliant and relevant idea

I had figured that the article was probably all we were going to get in terms of media. But just after 8am, BBC Radio Norfolk arrived and I was on the air live, just as lots of the councillors would have been driving in.[9] Then another press photographer turned up. And a TV crew. And they asked when all the children were going to arrive. And I didn't know because I still didn't know whether the teacher from Heacham had bottled it or not but I explained that it was quite a long way to Heacham, so I was sure they would be here soon.

In the meantime, pictures were taken and video recorded of the handful of pre-school children and their parents who had arrived from Melton Constable, including Karen.

---

for a field trip. What could be more important than teaching children about their right to protest and to have their voices heard? I'm sure the architects of the national curriculum didn't mean for it to become such a dire, hideous, joy-defeating and subversive straightjacket. But I hope my son gets to be taught by someone like this teacher, as Heacham is a bit far away to travel to.

[9] All sorts of people listen to local radio but in particular councillors on the way to the council.

We didn't notice the arrival of the children from Heacham at first because it just looked like a coach had pulled up at the bottom of the steps up to the council building. We did not notice the children getting off the coach because they were all too small for us to see them from where we were standing. But then we started to hear them chanting, and they appeared over the top of the steps like a mini armada: waving placards and repeating their slogan.

As things that happen on the steps of County Hall go, it was absolutely breath-taking. The pictures are hilarious. And as the children filed into the committee room itself where the meeting was beginning, the media all followed too.

There were not enough seats for the children in the committee room so they went and sat on the floor outside and ate picnics from their lunchboxes. It was incredibly civilised. What impressed me most was that all the tiny children knew exactly why they were there: they understood that the council were planning to take away their lollipop lady, and that she was there to protect them crossing the road.

They also understood that the councillors were making the decision in the next room. I know all this because BBC Radio Norfolk interviewed some of them and I heard it while I was driving home. I really hope more teachers do field trips like this in the future, and that the Heacham area has in waiting some politically experienced, active and successful campaigners that will transform West Norfolk in years to come.

When the decision was announced that the committee had overturned its own recommend-ation in the case of all 38 sites, a huge chorus of tiny voices cheered. I felt satisfaction that no single experience in business has ever provided me with. At that point I knew I absolutely had to win the election campaign I was about to start fighting, because campaigning and standing up to power is what I wanted to do with my life.

The next day we were on the front page of the *Eastern Daily Press*: 'JOY AT LOLLIPOP REPRIEVE'. I realised that my first successful campaign would also be one of the most important ingredients of the election campaign to come. It also proved to me that if there is one thing all politicians fear, it is bad press – and the sort of press that a five-year-old generates from telling people they are scared is about the most dangerous sort there is.

The whole experience reminded me of something I have known for a long time: if you do a good thing in a good way, people will want to help.

4
The (not so) glamorous world of local politics
(Freya)

If you have never been involved in local election campaigning before, you would be forgiven for thinking that it's filled with debates about park benches and leafleting in the rain. You wouldn't be too far wrong on either count: local election campaigning, and perhaps local politics in general, is not for glamour-seekers.

This is a lesson that was learned the hard way early on when a good friend joined our campaign. They had a lot of good ideas for how to brand-buff Steff and sell his hairstyle as this century's next 'big thing', and his emotional support of Steff mattered a lot for building the early foundations of the campaign.

The trouble was that he is, to coin a phrase, a bit of a hipster (a missing segment in Chris Rose's Values Based Segmentation model, perhaps) and as such, saw the campaign through that lens. As much as I love Melton Constable, it's not the place celebrities rush to with their Instagram accounts.

So where he wanted a Twitter feed filled by images of Steff posing with glamorous 'youth voters' or basking in sun-drenched pubs, the reality was more about normal people who wanted to talk about things like potholes and healthcare provision, and frazzled parents pissed off by decades of abysmal (read: non-existent) bus services. And this required us to talk to them in person, mostly in grey weather, because leafleting schedules do not care to liaise with the weather gods.

Thus, although this friend's initial role was to be in charge of Brand Steff, we quickly realised that going out on a Saturday in the rain with community surveys that leak ink onto your thumbs was going to be significantly more important than tweeting. It quickly became apparent that he was not particularly keen on any of the following, especially in combination: bad weather, rural Norfolk, leaflets which leak ink onto your thumbs, the general public.

Our friend is a brilliant brainstormer, a talented ideas-man and genuinely savvy with social media. But for someone to be at the heart of the campaign, they have to *be* at the heart of it: it is all or nothing. I needed people who knew who Alan the sign guy was and who had his number to hand, who understood the ins and outs of the lollipop lady campaign, and who could remember the name of the family that own the butcher's shop.

The lesson here for all of us was that, to be a core member of a campaign team, you have to be regularly at the coal-face, because otherwise you simply lose track of the plot. And staying on top of the weirdly twisting narrative is half the battle.

Sometimes I hear people say that they are more interested in parliamentary-level than local-level campaigning, probably because they imagine that it is more exciting and glitzy. But in terms of what is required to win, parliamentary campaigns are not much different from local ones. Sure: there's a larger geographical area to grapple with, and the issues can be juicier, but you still have to pound the tarmac and wear out your knuckles on thousands of doors.

In the most recent general election, for Norman Lamb's campaign, only the campaign manager and his second-in-command were exempt from door-stepping; everybody from Norman's parliamentary staff team down to the newest, most inexperienced volunteers were lumped together in canvass teams and let loose on the election-weary residents of rural Norfolk.

There are few campaign team roles so

important that they don't entail a significant amount of time being a doorstep warrior with the rank and file.

And this is because, when it comes to election campaigns, there is simply no replacement for talking to humans. And when it comes to talking to humans – even, astonishingly, in the twenty-first century – there is no replacement for talking to them face to face. You can gather voters together at coffee mornings or hustings events, but a sure-fire way to help them realise you give a damn about their priorities, and to give them a forum for a feedback, is to knock on their doors.

One of the things our friend did, however, was find Tim, who became our literature design guy. Tim *could* limit his involvement because he wasn't going to have an input on the campaign strategy stuff (of which brand and social media are definitely a part). Steff and I discussed the messaging, Steff drafted the copy, and Tim made sure the design and the content were singing from the same song sheet.

The freshness of Tim's input and his creative expertise were a real asset, and made our leaflets stand out from the crowd.

Potholes versus the bigger picture

I want to add a quick side note to the issue of

excitement and glamour in campaigning, because the full picture is not just about people being disappointed that campaigns involve more delivering-in-the-drizzle than attractively sipping G&Ts in rustic pubs. It is also about a concern I have heard from people who genuinely want to change the world, but are afraid that local election campaigns do not touch on the issues that 'really matter' and are therefore not worth a serious activist's time.

I thought about this a lot over the course of the campaign. Here I was, pouring practically all my spare time and energy over the course of several months into the single mission of getting one person elected to local government where there was little chance of them being part of the governing party even if they won. If it had not been that the candidate was my brother, would I have felt that it was a good use of human resources?

First of all, for the record, the perception that local politics skips over all the juicy issues is a little unfair. I was surprised at how often we discussed issues as wide-ranging as immigration, foreign aid, tuition fees, education, and climate change on the doorstep. But the reality remains that a lot of the chat is about issues of a seemingly 'lower order': GP waiting times, the frequency of the buses, that dangerous road by the school and, yes, potholes.

There are lots of ways to make change. Protests and pressure groups, direct action and lobbying for legal change, civil disobedience and radical literature are all vital – their emancipatory and transformative effects should never be underestimated. But making a difference to people's everyday lives also needs hard-working, emotionally intelligent people in politics at all levels of government.

Many of the problems that families face today cannot be resolved by a revolution ten years down the line. The infamously dire state of Children's Services at Norfolk County Council – and the individuals and families that have been put through hell as a result of its widely-documented inadequacies – is surely a case in point.[10]

Moreover, there is no point changing principles if there is no one decent around to enact them, and protect them from u-turns and vested interests. Even radical changes have more trivial

---

[10] At the time of writing, happily, Norfolk County Council has just managed to get an improved Ofsted report and appoint a permanent director of Children's Services.

manifestations at an everyday level; we might pass legislation ensuring parity of funding for mental health in Parliament, but if local representatives do not hold devolved spending to account, or keep an eye on the quality of service delivery on the ground, such an important change in principle may not play out in practice.

Policy does not exist in a vacuum – even the most dramatic shifts have their everyday manifestations. The introduction of the welfare state was arguably one of the most transformative moments in British society. But anyone who has ever gone through the stigma-laden hell of receiving jobseeker's allowance, or attending a disability living allowance assessment, knows that it *matters* who your representative is when you run into difficulties or fall through the net – just like it matters who is sitting across from you at a job centre.

Finally, it is questionable how you can politically empower the indifferent or the disenfranchised if they don't see politics working for them *even* at a local level? Councillors – like MPs – have a great deal of discretion over how much they bother to help people, and how much time they give time to people's requests, ideas and interests. The councillor who makes the effort to help the couple who have been sent in circles by local bureaucracy over a fostering issue, or the person whose sister is being let down by mental health service provision, or the young people who want a decent skate park, or the family in the house by the pub who just want the lines repainted around their designated parking space to stop tourists parking in it – will start to be seen as someone who actually gives a damn.

Because, for the voter who has been routinely ignored by their representatives, that bus shelter that has *never* been repaired, despite repeated requests, represents so much more than a bus shelter: it represents the arrogance and laziness of the political class.

One of the reasons Norman Lamb has been so successful is because people found something to believe in, to be optimistic about: they may not agree with all of his political value base, but they see him as a politician prepared to stand up for them when the odds are stacked against them. I saw this when I was a caseworker and read hundreds of letters from constituents, thanking Norman for his help in achieving sometimes life-transforming change.

When, two days after polling day, a woman told me that, thanks to Steff's help with her daughter's employment situation, her daughter and her husband – both in their early 30s – had gone out to vote for the first time in their lives, I knew we were on the right track. If empowering someone to vote for the first time in their life isn't radical, I don't know what is.

I know first-hand how bloody hard it is to believe you are 'being radical' when you have traipsed around a housing estate for four hours asking people to fill in surveys and being met largely with disdain or indifference. That is where the energy you felt while driving, listening to loud, dramatic music and dreaming of a world of political harmony starts to fade, the drizzle begins, and you think with grim resignation about the prospect of eating your packed lunch in the car.

But if you feel like your calling is local government, or if you are dreaming of revolution and wondering whether you are wasting your time with a county council campaign, I urge you to hold on to those moments – however small – of genuine transformation, to remember the person who tells you no politician has ever knocked on their door before, who says they voted for the first time that day because of you.

5
Training
(Steff)

There are two points to this chapter. One links this story to my professional background and the other talks about one of the things I think made a big difference to my campaign: the training programme I ran in North Norfolk.[11]

The training programme had a very boring title: 'Candidates 2017' (quite unlike "<u>MELTON CONSTABLE: getting to WIN</u>"). But people showed up, and we covered topics like 'Campaign planning and Teambuilding', 'The numbers' (fundraising, and using electoral data), 'How to

---

[11] I really hope it made a difference to some of the other candidates too, some of whom only came to one or two sessions, and a few of whom turned up to the whole programme. Lots of people learn by doing (including me) and I also think that, if you know something, then leading or going on training about it is a great way to force yourself to do it – and avoid being a cobbler with no shoes.

write words that win' and 'Having a consistent message'.

I think the biggest difference the training made was by putting the idea on the table that we were doing something that could be trained *for* - something that could be improved on, and wasn't just down to luck. The content was basically what I knew from a career in communications, through the lens of Ed Maxfield and Mark Pack's book *101 Ways to Win an Election*.

I've often been left frustrated by party training - with the exception of some of ALDC's[12] work - and wondering who on earth it is catering for. "This is Twitter, it's really important you're on Twitter, to retweet press this," said one of the highlights that stood out. So, I thought: there must be a better way of doing this, and I'm going to do it.

Luckily North Norfolk Lib Dems was willing to be cajoled into the role of guinea pig. At this stage they knew very little about me other than that I

---

[12] The Association of Liberal Democrat Councillors, where one of our excellent external speakers was from. They know a thing or two about campaigning and training and joining up before you become a candidate is well worth the small amount of money it costs.

had been elected as vice chair of the local party, and persuaded a select handful of people that having a Big, Hairy, Audacious Goal (BHAG) and making it happen through community politics was a better way of standing out from the crowd than posing by potholes (this is work in progress and the subject of quite another book).

People like Ed Maxfield were really in favour of holding training, which was big of him because I knew he had probably already spent the last fifteen years trying to get people to listen to exactly the same things we were going to talk about.

I am under no apprehension that the decisions to elect me to be vice chair, invest in training and agree to a ridiculous BHAG were the reason we won seven out of thirteen county seats in North Norfolk. But they were part of a wider set of decisions by Ed, local party chair Denys and others, that I think have changed the course of the local party, from being the 'keep Norman Lamb elected party' (something it is biologically impossible to do forever), to one which is in a strong position to take over a serious amount of North Norfolk in 2019.

Another thing that I realised was different – which these people helped instigate – was the employment of Sarah Tustin (shared with and half funded by, I should say, the excellent folk at Broadland Lib Dems, who also held two of their seats). Sarah is a hugely energetic, brilliantly sharp and highly capable organiser. She brought many new skills to the team when she joined to help fight the county council campaign, including proper coffee, which she brought to the first training session.

I found the training from external people particularly eye-opening. We had excellent contributions from 'our own' in Norfolk as well as from further afield and my faith in the Liberals reached an all-time high because of this: there are, I concluded, people out there in the party who are experienced, professional and properly liberal, who don't have their heads stuck in the sand or their eyes closed about why hardly anyone votes for us as a party.

The most striking of these actually came from an outsider, albeit a sympathiser: Chris Rose, who used to be programme director for Greenpeace. Alongside his lifelong experience working on campaigns – both party political and issue-based – Chris is author of the book *What Makes People Tick: The Three Hidden Worlds of Settlers, Prospectors and Pioneers*. The book explains how different societal groups see the world through different lenses and, in particular, how people's values are influenced by different unconscious drivers.

Drawing on the 'Values-Based Segmentation' model at the core of the book, Chris helped us, through discussion and practical exercises, to put ourselves in the shoes of voters with potentially very different world views from our own, and to try to shape our messaging to resonate with their values.[13]

The power of this model to account for some of the surprising election results we have experienced recently blew my mind. Chris also spoke with a quiet, sardonic tone that made me laugh a lot because it was clear he knew exactly what he was talking about and didn't need to sell it, whereas I spend a lot of time doing talks and running workshops on things no one really knows the precise answer to, and I always use an over-zealous approach to fudging over any grey areas.

Talking of which: this seems like a good time to

---

[13] You can find out more about the Values Base Segmentation model at www.cultdyn.co.uk and there is a list of papers, sources and studies at http://threeworlds.campaignstrategy.org/?p=1420 (see also more recent blog posts, especially on Brexit).

bring up what I was doing before I decided to become county councillor for Melton Constable. I haven't really had a proper job since I was eighteen when I ran a beautiful inn called the Buckinghamshire Arms in Norfolk. And I only did that because I heard that nine other people had tried to run it so far that year.

Since then, I have been a self-styled entrepreneur. There isn't really any other type of entrepreneur: no one I know has ever been approached by someone who says "you seem like a smart, capable person, will you be our 'entrepreneur'?" It's a job title you can only ever give yourself.

Thankfully this isn't an autobiography so let's just say that, like all proper entrepreneurs, I have started a few businesses, and they have been mixed. What I have always really wanted to do is be a politician. It is an awful thing to admit: but it is true.

I didn't want to be one of those politicians who wore a rosette from birth, though. It makes me feel slightly ill when Liberal Democrats talk about how 'they were heady days, back when I was a student, or president of the Young Liberals, or trying to persuade the other toddlers of the merits of the 'Single Transferrable Vote'.

"What have you actually done?" I scream,

silently. So I thought I had better go and do something. I went out and, in summary: hired about 200 people in total, raised £2m in venture capital, started two technology companies, ran a large film post-production facility, worked with lots of different sized teams, did consulting for some huge brands, created some much smaller ones, made a feature-length romantic comedy, took a disgusting thirty six flights in a year doing talks about the Internet, and failed, miserably and completely, in about every single way it is possible to fail without going to prison.

I felt this was starting to set me up quite well for politics, which is why Ed Maxfield was able to persuade me to get involved when he did.

Oh yes, and training: I've done quite a bit of training. Some lovely people at a company called Econsultancy have always been willing to put me back on the books when I come crawling because the latest mad venture to change the way the world does something has failed. Which is extremely lucky as it means I have been able to maintain a standard of living and have a family.

6
Training and jargon
(Freya)

I remember things really started to kick off when the training began. That was when I realised that we had no plan, and that we badly needed one.

In mid-December, Steff got all the candidates for the 2017 county elections together, plus random sidekicks, like me and Dave.[14] We were grouped in the conference room at the North Norfolk constituency office, crowded around a

---

[14] I have reached a conclusion about Dave – which I have voiced to him – which is that he must be certifiably unhinged, because he voluntarily gives up inordinate amounts of his free time slaving away for Liberal Democrat candidates, for little reward, and without a whisper of resentment. His 'delivery selfies' – which he takes every time he goes out leafleting – are a photographic homage to the graft of all those quiet stoics upon whom successful campaigns rely. It is so important to have someone like this who you can run to in a crisis.

table with every single chair we could get our hands on, armed with coffee and biscuits, and surrounded by trailing projector wires and teetering piles of unfolded Focus leaflets. It was truly the perfect starting image for a farcical film about local politics.[15]

As Steff has said, these gatherings were imaginatively called *Candidates 2017* and the purpose of them was:

a) to help alleviate all the campaign suffering through the injection of community spirit, and
b) to help more seasoned campaigners pass on their wisdom to newbies, as well as to inspire all – both old hands and new – via external speakers.

The sessions petered out towards the end of February when the campaign got into full swing and people's time was taken up with door-

---

[15] For genuinely brilliant TV about the farcical nature of local politics, see US comedy series *Parks and Recreation*. It will help you learn to laugh in a devil-may-care manner when you have a thousand envelopes that need to be hand-delivered to remote parts of the division by Tuesday and you have driven your car into a ford.

knocking and panic. But they were an incredibly effective way to get everyone started, and to provide a space for people to feel they were actually part of something.

Too often, new candidates are talked into standing locally with promises of the joys of campaigning and the fulfillment of collective effort. Then they are abandoned to the winding lanes and housing estates of their allocated patch, with a startlingly yellow rosette and clipboard, and expected somehow to sustain the will to knock on strangers' doors for six hours at a time.

I am convinced that the best music, coffee or gin in the world cannot substitute for the motivation of group membership. In particular, I think it highly likely that, if a candidate loses, they are going to be more willing to stand again if the experience has not been wholly lonely and painful.

There are so many small ways you can help foster a sense of community around a campaign effort. Socials in pubs are great, as are Facebook groups or message threads where people can share their frustrating or hilarious experiences or ask questions. But the particularly effective feature of the 'Candidates 2017' training programme was that it served a tangible, practical purpose – which helped motivate us all to turn up, while also creating a social space for building relationships. Another great thing about the sessions was that they helped get new campaigners up to pace on the cult-like campaign jargon used by Liberal Democrats nationwide.

Funnily enough, the internet yields astonishingly few results when you try googling something like 'what is a Lib Dem Blue Letter?'. So, to save other newcomers from suffering entire conversations in which they have no idea what anyone is talking about, below is a list of some of the most commonly used words and phrases in campaigns:

Campaign literature - simply refers to all bits of paper pushed through letterboxes during the campaign, whether by volunteers, or a courier like UK Mail or Royal Mail.

Impressum or *Insert* - the footer legally required on all party-political literature or addenda (including, for instance, things you put in the window of your car, basket of your bike, back of your T-shirt or delivery bag which are overtly campaign-related). Check with your local office for the most up-to-date wording, but it is usually something along the lines of 'Printed, published and promoted by [insert name of local head of campaigns] on behalf of the Liberal Democrats, [insert address of local party office]'. It is a classic rookie error to forget to put the legal insert on your campaign materials. I have heard horror stories of, er, people (definitely not me and Steff) forgetting to put the insert on 'sorry we missed you' cards and having to stick labels onto a thousand cards manually before they could go out door-knocking...

Mailshot - a mass mailing, usually in the form of an email or a leaflet or letter delivered to voters by courier, as opposed to volunteers. These are much more common in general election campaigns where there is the budget for mass deliveries and many more people to reach.

Tabloid - a word many are surprised to see anywhere near liberal campaigners. In fact, 'tabloid' in this context refers not to the horrors of the actual red-top news industry, but to a piece of literature sneakily designed to look like a local community newspaper. The only similarity is the cringe-worthy headlines designed to catch the voters' attention, such as 'TORIES EXPOSED FOR SCANDALOUS [insert local grievance for which Tory-led council is responsible]'. Tabloids are usually sent out early on, to lay the foundations for the campaign. In our area, for instance, the early tabloids usually feature something to do with Norman Lamb (because he is so widely liked) followed by an article about the local candidate.

Focus leaflet - the 2016 *Guardian* obituary for Sir Trevor Jones, the Liberal Party councillor and campaigner who popularised the use of the Focus leaflet, describes is at "the brash leaflet based on local issues that electors identified with – that is still ubiquitous for Lib Dems". Indeed, Focus leaflets still form the backbone of Lib Dem campaign literature today. Apart from the word 'Focus' across the top, the leaflets vary enormously in style and content but, broadly speaking, they identify local community issues and discuss how the candidate is taking action in response.

Blue Letter - Chris Rennard is often hailed as the founding father of Lib Dem leaflet strategy, and in his capacity as Director of Campaigns and Elections and later Chief Executive of the party, he invented various formats for campaign literature which survive to this day, including 'blue ink letters', generally shortened to 'blue letters'.[16] The letters were first used by campaigners in the 1980s and were handwritten with dark blue ink onto lighter blue paper (hence the name) before being photocopied umpteen times and placed in individually hand-addressed envelopes. Today, our local party more often uses white paper, but the basic idea remains the same: to produce a piece of literature sufficiently personalised for the voter actually to open and read it.

Street letter - unlike a piece of generic literature sent to all voters, these are generally targeted at a specific village or town or even a particular subsection of that community, and relate to an issue affecting them only. A classic example would be a flooding problem on a particular road. Having taken action to address the issue, the candidate might send a letter to the fifty or so affected residents, explaining their involvement and promising to keep them updated on any progress. In our campaign, Steff sent a street letter to residents in the two villages affected by

---

[16] See Mark Pack's excellent summary of the history of Lib Dem campaigning for more info: http://bit.ly/2gauCk6

the school crossing issue, co-signed by a local parent, explaining the outcome of the County Hall committee meeting and congratulating the community on its success.

Canvass sheets - the printed sheets produced by Connect (see below) for door-knockers, containing the names and addresses of the people to be contacted, as well as their Voter ID (also see below). Note that these sheets constitute triple A class sensitive data and *must be shredded* once you have finished processing them.

A3 leaflet - I remember being slightly bewildered when first hearing about A3 leaflets. How on earth could it be practical to push something that huge through a letterbox? As it turns out, A3 leaflets are obviously folded. They are useful because of the amount of information they can hold. We did an A3 'glossy' leaflet – produced by an external printers – as our last major leaflet of the campaign. We used the vast inside space to list all our campaign achievements as well as a list of manifesto-type promises. We also listed lots of lovely quotes from local residents (with their permission, of course) about Steff.

Riso - this is an old-school but highly cost-effective industrial-sized printer that can reel off two-tone leaflets at astonishing speed. It is a favourite of Lib Dem local party offices nationwide. It is also responsible for that ink that comes off on your hands.

Good mornings - this is actually an invention of the Liberal Party, prior to the merger with the Social Democratic Party in 1988. They are a simple leaflet that says something along the lines of 'Good Morning - it's Polling Day' and are delivered at an ungodly hour in the morning so as to catch voters before they go off to work. We began delivering ours at the relatively civilised time of 6.15am, though I have known of people starting as early as 5am to maximise coverage. Creeping up people's driveways and praying they don't have a dog that will wake up the whole street as you slip your hand into their letterbox is one of the few legal insights into a career of burglary you will ever have.

Eve of polls - similar to Good Morning leaflets, in that their major purpose is to remind your voter base about polling day, but delivered the night before. If you have a serious amount of personpower available to you, you might want to consider doing both to every non-outlying household. Around a week before polling day we began delivering addressed envelopes containing a post-it note on which we had stamped 'Don't Forget to Vote on May 4th', which we encouraged people to put on their fridges. As per usual, this took us much longer to produce and deliver than we had anticipated, and we were still delivering the remnants the night before polling day. We therefore decided not to deliver Eve of Polls (unless we'd stayed up all night, it would have been impossible) and instead to just deliver Good Mornings to a few target locations.

Connect - Connect is the online software used by the Lib Dems to store data on campaigns and voters. It is an excellent resource, once you get your head around its sometimes less-than-friendly user interface. You can think of Connect as the electoral register overlaid with information collected specifically by the party. It includes, for instance, everyone registered to vote in your area.[17] They will all have a profile on Connect

---

[17] Except people who have removed themselves from the electoral register. Some people - such as vulnerable adults or people under witness protection schemes - are not on the electoral register but are nonetheless

containing their name and address. Any further information collected by the party, such as a phone number, email address and answers to doorstep or survey questions (relating to everything from party political affiliation to their views on specific issues like the EU) will also be recorded. Connect also has a handy maps feature, allowing you to carve up the constituency, electoral division or ward into delivery or door-knocking routes called 'walks'. Connect is what is used to produce door-knocking sheets and delivery round maps, as well as to crunch the numbers in your area.[18] To get a Connect account you will need to speak with whoever is in charge of Connect at your local party office, as access is – for obvious reasons – tightly controlled.

---

registered to vote.

[18] For instance, we used Connect right at the beginning of the campaign to tell us how what proportion of the electorate was aligned with different parties. We then refined that search to only include people who had been asked about their voting preferences in the last five years (to remove more out-of-date information). We could also use Connect to find out how many email addresses and phone numbers we had, or how many voters we had listed as under the age of 30.

Minivan - the app used in lieu of paper canvassing sheets. Minivan is a bit like a portable Connect: it allows for lists of voters and all their info to be downloaded from Connect, along with digital maps showing you where doors are located, and used on the go. Minivan needs the internet to download the list but, once that is done, you can input data from your door-knocking with no signal or wifi. Data is simply saved on your phone until you reconnect to the internet, at which point you can 'sync' using a small button on the screen. Once you get used to the absence of paper sheets, Minivan is an absolute life-saver. Just one word of advice: do purchase a portable battery charger for your phone, as Minivan drains juice like there's no tomorrow.

Voter ID - refers to a voter's party political affiliation, as determined by Connect. Every time a particular voter ticks a box about party preference on a survey, or speaks to someone on the doorstep or on the phone, that data is processed according to Connect's algorithm, which figures out roughly where that person is situated on the political spectrum. A person's voter ID is therefore much more than simply what they last told us. If someone has said repeatedly that they vote Lib Dem, then they will be listed as a Lib Dem, or even a Strong Lib Dem. If, however, back in 2010 they told us on the doorstep they usually vote Labour, and then told us last week that they are planning to vote Lib Dem in the local election, then they are more likely to be listed as a 'Red Lib Dem' or 'Soft Labour' (see below).

No datas - pretty much what it says on the tin: people about whom we have no information regarding their voting history or party alignment.

Weak Lib Dem - I have come across new volunteers who are thoroughly outraged when they discover that they themselves have been categorised on Connect as a 'Weak Lib Dem'. But as much as the term conjures up images of socks-and-sandal-wearing woolly liberals with dangerously low blood sugar, a Weak Lib Dem is in fact either someone who has told us, at some point, that they vote Lib Dem but about whom we have no further information to confirm their alignment, or someone who has repeatedly told us that they are sympathetic but doubtful about the party. That is, it means their affiliation with the party is weak rather than strong.

Soft Con - stands for 'Soft Conservative', and refers to a voter who is generally aligned with the

Conservative party but who is sympathetic to Lib Dem policies and ideals and might, therefore, be convinced to vote for us.

Soft Lab - same as above, only Labour.

Red/Blue Lib Dems - these voters are subtly different from 'softs'. Whereas a Soft Conservative, say, is primarily a Conservative voter who might be persuaded to vote Lib Dem, a Blue Lib Dem by contrast is primarily a Lib Dem voter but with Conservative-leaning views. In the same way, a Red Lib Dem is a Lib Dem voter who leans more towards the Left.

Swing/Squeeze - this phrase refers to a group of more 'on the fence' voters whose support we might be able to scoop up with the right message or strategy. Which group of people are referred to as 'squeeze' voters and which as 'swing' depends on the political leanings of your area. Norfolk, excluding Norwich, is what is called 'Tory-facing', in that the general political leaning is Conservative. In most election battles here, the Conservatives are our main opposition. In these areas, the 'squeeze' voters are those who you can persuade to support you by calling for a tactical vote. In our case, these were Labour-sympathetic voters to whom we pointed out that Labour couldn't win, and that their vote would be better spent helping us to keep the Tories out. In essence you are 'squeezing' these voters to your side via the threat of their least favourite party winning. Swing voters are those who lean towards the main opposition. They cannot be won over by the same appeal to tactical voting, because they know the party they definitely don't support won't win. Rather, you have to convince them to 'swing' their preference towards you rather than their habitual candidate. You might do this by having a reasoned debate about values, in which they discover that the Liberal Democrats uphold their philosophical priorities after all. You are more likely to do it by gaining their approval through being seen to be the most hard-working and trustworthy candidate.

Probs and Defs - this is the phrase used to refer to the core base of likely Lib Dem voters. It generally includes people categorised as 'weak Lib Dem' or Blue/Red Lib Dem (all the 'probables', in other words) as well as all those down in Connect as either 'Lib Dem' or 'Strong Lib Dem'. When you run canvass analysis, the number of probs and defs is an important gauge of how you are doing. You are always likely to have more probs and defs as a percentage of people whose Voter ID you have because your supporters are always more likely to tell you their allegiance than anyone else. So when we were running at 60 per cent "prob and def" close to the election, we knew we were in with a good chance. Every area will be different and we took 45 per cent of the vote in the end – Norfolk has a lot of secret Conservative voters.

Stay at homes - this term refers to a group of people who, it is generally accepted, are extremely unlikely to vote for us. This means that we have strong evidence that they are staunch opposition voters and we would, in fact, prefer it if they forgot there was an election altogether. Hence, they are generally removed from canvassing lists either from day one or at least from early on in the campaign.[19] They are especially removed from

_____

[19] We left in all voters for our surveying and for about the first month of our door-knocking. It is important, I think, to allow for the possibility that some of these people may have changed their minds since they were last asked about their voting preferences (especially if the last time they were asked was 2001). It is also always possible that, by engaging with them positively, you may help to change their mind. Admittedly, as

polling day GOTV operations (see below), in the hope that they will literally 'stay at home' on polling day.

Historical poster site - on Connect, there is a list of people who have, in the past, agreed to have a Lib Dem poster board or garden poster (these refer to the same thing) outside their house. Sometimes, though, the last time they had a poster board was literally decades ago, so there is a distinction between actual poster sites – people who have been asked over the course of the *current campaign* and have agreed to have a poster – and *historical* poster sites. These historical sites generally need to be contacted to check whether they are okay with having one this time round.

---

admirable as it is to maintain this kind of optimism, it is extremely rare that I have had a positive response from someone previously recorded as a staunch UKIP or Conservative voter on the doorstep in North Norfolk. Much of the time it does rather feel like you are wasting precious time you could be spending with people who are not filled with rage by the sight of your yellow badge.

GOTV - this stands for 'Get Out The Vote' but is also amusingly referred to as 'knocking up' so don't be confused when someone tells you that they've knocked up Mrs Tibbs at No. 44 and she's due at the polling station at 5pm. You can spend months building up supporters, but if they fail to show up on polling day then all that work will have been pointless. GOTV is mostly done in the few days running up to polling day as well as, of course, polling day itself. It is about making sure that people are so heartily sick of being reminded when polling day is that they can't possibly wake up on Thursday morning and decide to go on a spontaneous holiday, spend all day gardening, or be ill, because they are so full of electoral enthusiasm.[20]

Shuttleworth - the list of voters targeted by GOTV operations on polling day, generally filtered to include only likely supporters or sometimes squeeze voters. The Shuttleworth is amended throughout the day by door-knocking and telling

---

[20] If you're fortunate enough for your polling day to be May 4, as it was for us, then you also get to infuriate people by saying *May the Fourth Be With You* 4,000 times in the preceding weeks.

data, so that the list shrinks to include only those who have not yet voted or who have not yet been contacted. Shuttleworths get their name from an obscure historical anecdote which, for the geekier among you, can be read about on the *Lib Dem Voice* website.[21]

Telling - the practice of sitting outside a polling station asking people for their polling card numbers. The purpose of this is not to find out *how* people voted, but rather to note down that they *have* voted, so that we don't waste time knocking on their door to remind them to go and vote. People often don't bother with telling for local elections, as it doesn't always turn out to be an effective use of resources – it has to save more volunteer time than it takes to have someone sat there (and someone else collecting in the data and re-running the lists). Of course, if a volunteer is unable knock on doors or unwilling to do phone canvassing, then it is hugely useful to get them to do telling at one of the larger polling stations in your area.

---

[21] http://www.libdemvoice.org/how-did-shuttleworths-get-their-name-40299.html

Committee room **-** the room used on polling day as a 'base' for operations.

Election agent - the person appointed by the candidate or local party to make sure the campaign complies with the law. This is usually somebody with prior experience and knowledge of election law, in our case, Ed Maxfield.

Constituency, division, ward - these are the terms used to refer to a particular candidate's area or 'patch' – the area she or he is campaigning to win. Parliamentary candidates run for constituency seats, county council candidates run in electoral divisions, and district or city councillors run in wards. They all overlap and tessellate and constitute one another in bizarre and confusing ways. For instance, Steff's electoral division, Melton Constable, straddled two separate constituencies: North Norfolk (held by Norman Lamb) and Broadland (held by a Conservative). This meant we had to be very careful about remembering not to say 'I am a volunteer for your local MP Norman Lamb' when knocking on villages in the Broadland constituency. The division was also made up of four district wards, only one of which – Astley ward – was held by a Liberal Democrat. Again, this meant carefully tailoring our messaging. So, for instance, we included a message from the district councillor for Astley in our Focus leaflet delivered to the villages in his ward, but sent a generic one elsewhere.

7
The master plan
(Freya)

To return to the discovery I highlighted at the start of the previous chapter: the training sessions were perhaps most significant for us because they prompted us to draft an achievable campaign plan early on. The fact remains that, for all my scepticism about inflexible, die-hard views on 'how campaigns should be run', there are certain tried and tested ideas about when certain things should ideally happen, and tapping into this existing knowledge is vital.

I remember spending a good three days poring over Google Spreadsheets, trying to make sense of the various deadlines and interlocking strands of the campaign that I had been told needed to be included, and fitted around various non-negotiable dates (such as nominations form deadlines, the postal voter application deadline, the election spending period and, er, polling day itself).

It is like doing a jigsaw when about three quarters of the pieces are yet to be revealed, and you are perpetually comparing yourself to the perfectly assembled, shiny puzzles of the past, built by the more seasoned campaigners around you, who evidently 'did something right last time' but who can only really tell you what that was in snippets of anecdotal conversation.

One thing I do know is that, even if the plan evolves as you go, having some sense of roughly when you are aiming to do things doesn't half help, not least because it breaks down the overwhelming list of stuff to be done into more clearly discernible tasks and problems. It also exposes where a lot of the gaps are in time to fill them. For example, how are we going to find a vehicle to fit signboards into? Who can set up my Connect account? Does the office have envelopes we can use or do we need to be responsible for ordering those ourselves? Does the envelope-stuffing machine work?[22] And what kinds of people you are going to need, when, where and in

---

[22] Answer: sort of. But it can't cope with putting envelopes inside envelopes, as we discovered to the great displeasure of our long-suffering mother and her partner Bill, who then spent three days helping me hand-stuff 1,500 postal vote application forms with freepost return envelopes.

what numbers, to help implement the 'to do' list.

I am undecided about how useful being given a full campaign plan template would have been (as opposed to what we *were* given, which was lots of general but nonetheless useful conversational advice about roughly what to include). On the one hand, it would have avoided quite a lot of backtracking and mind-changing. On the other hand, it might have restricted our creative thinking. It might also have been bewildering; certainly, there was one point where I asked a handful of different, more experienced people how they thought we should order and implement our postal voter strategy and received five totally contrasting answers. This is more confusing than helpful.

For our plan, Steff and I used Google spreadsheets. This allowed us to have a live and editable version which both of us could easily access and amend online.

We split our plan up into three 'phases': the first and longest was the yellow phase which began on January 1.[23] This was all about laying

---

[23] Before this, we had no official 'plan' but had nonetheless been campaigning on and off for a couple of months. It was during this pre-plan era that we

foundations. Our priorities for this phase were *visibility and name-recognition, local issue-gathering, collecting voter IDs.*

Phase 2, the orange phase, began halfway through March and continued right up to the start of polling week. By mid-March we hoped to have finished door-knocking in each village in the division so that we could return for a second time to knock up households who had been out the first time round. Our other priorities for the orange phase were *postal voter engagement and poster boards.*

The red phase, which began on the Monday of polling week right up to and including polling day itself, had only one priority: Get Out The Vote. When the actions on any particular day had been completed, we put them in green. This was not only satisfying, but also helped us keep on top of where we were running behind. Alongside   the priorities for each 'phase', specific events and

---

delivered our first piece of literature (a tabloid featuring Norman Lamb on local health provision and Steff on the mobile phone signal), collected feedback from surveys and cottoned on to the school crossing issue, allowing Steff to begin supporting local parents in their plan to fight the council's proposal.

deadlines were also written in to the plan:

We started by putting in any planned absences Steff or I would have over the following six months. This meant we knew well in advance what time we had to play with and knew, for instance, that Steff was unfortunately away on business for four days at the end of April – prime door-knocking time so close to the election, that we had to compensate for by redoubling our efforts earlier in the month.

We also planned, purposefully, to keep every single Sunday free from campaign activities. Not only did we believe this would help protect our sanity, but Steff and his wife had had a baby in October 2016. Protecting Sundays meant that Steff was able to be more available, even when the campaign got frantic. Astonishingly, we did manage to make sure that Steff, despite being consumed by campaign activities for at least 75 per cent of his waking hours every other day of the week, never actually did any campaigning on a Sunday.

Next, we put in the broad outline for our delivery plan. We made a list of all the leaflets, in rough consecutive order, that we wanted to deliver between then and the end of the campaign.

The list looked something like this:

First tabloid

Street letter about Astley School Crossing Patrol

Focus 1

Focus 2

Postal voter registration letter to supporters and swing/squeeze voters

Focus 3

Blue letter to non-postal voters

Good mornings

For each leaflet, we started with the non-negotiable end dates like the postal voter registration deadline, and worked backwards. We then asked ourselves the following four questions to figure out the placement of leaflet-related deadlines in our schedule:

1. By what date do we want each leaflet to be delivered by?

2. At what point do we need to *begin* delivering to get the leaflets delivered by that date?

3. By what date does Ed need to finish the digital version of the leaflet in order to print 4,000 copies in time for us to start delivering?[24],[25]

---

[24] You need to liaise with whoever at your local party

4. By what date does Tim, our design guy, need the copy for the leaflet in order to have time to do the artwork by the date we want the final product sent to Ed?

Of course, if it had just been the two of us, we

---

office is in charge of printing to answer this question. As the campaign progressed, and especially after the delightful news about an impending general election caused resources to be, understandably, diverted away from the local campaigns, we did more and more printing ourselves. Nonetheless, it's important you don't make assumptions about the availability of the local party office staff - keep them on your side by liaising with them early on about their requirements. [25] If you are going to get anything printed externally by a professional printers, then it is also worth asking them early on what their turnaround time is. It is also good to suss out whether there are printers with whom the party already has an existing relationship. We are fortunate enough in North Norfolk to have a fantastic ally in the form of Roger at Stalham Century Printing. We are forever indebted to him for the number of times he turned things around at supremely short notice, and for tolerating our increasingly frenzied attitude to leaflets.

would never have been able to fit it all in. When we wrote up our initial deadlines we gradually shortened the amount of time needed in response to question two, banking on the fact that we would gather some volunteers to help us. Thankfully, as the campaign proceeded, we *were* helped by an increasing number of extremely generous people, who gave up their evenings and weekends to push paper through doors.[26]

The only thing that having a large network of volunteers changed, however, was that we now had to allow time in the schedule for distributing leaflet bundles to our deliverers (sometimes called 'wholesaling'), while still allocating sufficient time to our priority canvassing locations, *and* do the remaining delivery, without ending up driving hundreds of miles in a single day or getting home at one in the morning.

Having roughly figured out the delivery stuff, we then put in the dates of all relevant parish council (PC) meetings. I made a spreadsheet of all the parish councils in the division.[27] This had the

---

[26] See chapter 13 for more on the delivery and volunteer network.

[27] One of the more light-hearted screw-ups of the campaign was when Steff went to Plumstead, on my

names of their clerks and secretaries and relevant email addresses and phone numbers. I then scoured every parish council website for details of their meeting dates. Luckily, many of these follow a consistent formula for their meeting times, such as 'the second Wednesday of every month', which meant we could note down all the dates which fell during the campaign period in one go.

We also put in any one-off community events like coffee mornings that we felt Steff ought to attend. Every time we visited a village, we photographed its community signboard. We uploaded the photos into a shared Dropbox folder, and I went through every few days and pulled out

---

assurance that there was a parish council meeting in the village hall that night, only to discover that there was no village hall to speak of. After driving around for a while trying to locate phone signal, Steff did some googling and then gave me a ring.

'Freya, you know that parish council meeting tonight?'

'Yes, what about it?'

'Well, you know how there are, in fact, *two* Plumsteads in Norfolk? One in North Norfolk and one about 25 miles away, just outside Norwich?'

'....... Oh s**t.'

the dates and details of any event that I thought ought to be fitted into the schedule. Anything I needed Steff to confirm (most new additions to the schedule, in other words) were put in red. Once confirmed, Steff would change the text colour to black.

We made a decision about halfway through the campaign, when our schedule was getting rather cluttered, that village coffee mornings and any other one-off events would be recorded in Steff's personal diary only, rather than the campaign schedule, to allow us to use the schedule primarily for the two key tasks of door-knocking and delivering, as well as other fundamentals.

Steff uses Google calendar for his personal diary, and he gave me access to it, which was extremely helpful, as it meant that whenever I wanted to add something to the campaign diary, I could check the viability against his personal schedule before marking it in red.

I thoroughly recommend anyone carrying out a campaign manager or similar role to make sure they have access to the candidate's personal diary. Steff was juggling work and part-time parenting a new baby in addition to the campaign, so it was not unusual for 90 per cent of his day to be accounted for. Knowing when he had spare time and where he was going to be geographically on any given day made designing a campaign plan which worked for both of us a hell of a lot easier, and it made handling changes in real-time much more efficient.

If, for instance, someone called me up offering to go door-knocking with Steff any Tuesday or Friday afternoon in the coming fortnight, or I got an email back from a new deliverer in a far-flung village who needed their bundle dropped off to them before they went away, I could swap around plans to accommodate these unexpected events with some level of certainty that they would fit with Steff's agenda.

I could, in other words, bypass Steff altogether in much of the diary-management. Having your finger on the pulse of the campaign in this way also means you can manage a lot of the campaign correspondence – for instance, with volunteers – without the candidate having to get involved.

On the door-knocking front, we eventually settled into a routine whereby, a few days prior to any given week, I would check up and amend the door-knocking schedule as appropriate, so that Steff could plan his activities and work around canvassing.

I kept a running record of our data in relation to each village. For instance, I kept a list of the number of households in each village, and how many doors remained un-knocked, so that I knew which were the larger, more densely populated areas as well as which areas we had neglected. I also kept a record of how many times we had visited each village and, importantly, on what days of the week. If you visit a particular village on a weekday, the people who are not at home are most likely people who work daytime on weekdays. So if and when you go to that village a second time, it makes sense to go on a Saturday to maximise your likelihood of rooting out these 'not-at-homes', and vice versa if you first went on a weekend.

A vast amount of key information for forming door-knocking strategy, particularly in areas where we had very little historic information, came from Connect's quite high-tech ability to use large amounts of centrally-entered socio-demographic data to identify likely sympathisers – even if we'd never spoken to them. Learning to use Connect is a must, although I actually found my way around it largely by trial and error, simply because I was having to learn on the job.

There are several tricks of the trade, however, without which you can end up wasting a lot of time and getting into a lot of confusing tangles. Asking someone familiar with the software to show you the ropes helps leapfrog a number of will-to-live-draining hours spent bashing your head against a laptop screen.

I found pinning up a map of the division on my bedroom wall helped enormously with getting my head around the area and the logistics of navigating it (for example, if Steff has an hour to fill on Wednesday morning after a coffee morning in Hindolveston, but he went door-knocking in Hindolveston just two days ago, knowing where is nearby that he can go and door-knock to make the most effective use of that hour).

If I have not already made it clear by now, campaign management is definitely a game for those who get a kick out of being mildly obsessive compulsive. I am not sure if I am proud or horrified to say that, on polling day, I bet Steff that I could name the Google maps driving-time estimation between any two villages in the division to within a minute.

This was a serious gamble but, happily for me, when Steff said 'okay, Great Ryburgh to Hindolveston', it paid off: it was, as I predicted, exactly 13 minutes.[28] Best free pint I've ever had.

The remaining fundamentals to note down in

---

[28] The fact that I resorted to estimating driving routes as a source of fun says quite a lot about my mental state that day, I think.

any schedule are signboards and phone banking. The signboards have several stages, which is why they need to be planned for in advance. You need to allow plenty of time for putting them up, as it takes longer than you think and some people only ask for boards once they see that other people have them, so you need to start getting them up nice and early to give yourself a chance to achieve a snowball effect. For phone-banking, you need to allow time for recruiting people to help you, or if you are doing it yourself, scheduling time in for it (I would aim for weekday evenings, which is time you are less likely to spend on doors).[29]

Inevitably, our deadlines changed as reality took hold. We never made the 'meet the

---

[29] I know plenty of people who disagree with this decision, but we didn't door-knock after about 6pm (except on polling day). We were normally knackered by that point because we had been out all day and, especially in the earlier months of the campaign, the light began to go around 6, and it felt a bit weird to be knocking on people's doors in semi-darkness. Maybe it's different in a city, where the lighting is better and there are more people around, but knocking on an old lady's door at 8pm in the middle of a tiny, silent village is unlikely, I think, to endear you to her.

candidate' video we had planned to release on Facebook, deciding instead that time on doors (we were behind schedule on canvassing) was more important than reaching out to the limited proportion of our voters who used social media.[30]

It also took us a lot longer to canvass every village than we had anticipated. Checking back over our plan, I see that we didn't actually start returning to villages for a second round until the end of March. Nonetheless, this still gave us a whole month for additional door-knocking. By this time, we had a much better idea of which villages were most time-effective and which were most likely to contain our supporters.

I also made decisions about where to go door-knocking on the basis of our previous levels of visibility in that area. In some villages, for instance, we had volunteers doing all the delivery rounds for us, whereas in others we did the delivery largely by ourselves. This meant that there were some villages where Steff's face was

---

[30] We did, later on, commission Tim to make a viral video aimed at the youth vote, which we used the paid-for Facebook advertising tool to promote. This was thanks to a generous donation from a friend, given specifically to reach out to younger voters.

better known, simply because of how the delivery rounds were distributed. So, when faced with a decision about where to go on a particular day, I would try to send Steff to places he hadn't often been to. By the end of the campaign we had been to every village on at least three separate occasions – and sometimes, as in the case of Briston, our largest village by far, well over twenty.

8

Residents' surveys

(Freya)

Earlier on, I talked about the importance of sounding people out about what they actually want for their communities. One very good way to do this is to knock on their doors. This is especially good for making individual people feel heard, and for gaining their trust and respect. But when you want to sample the opinions and 'hot issues' of a community at scale, a more efficient – if less 'in depth' – way to do this is through community surveys.

One common way of community surveying is through 'knock and drops'. This is where you knock on someone's door with the sole purpose of explaining to them that you are carrying out a survey. I would say something like 'Hi, I'm Freya, I'm just calling on behalf of my brother Steff/my friend Sarah/your local MP Norman Lamb because we're carrying out a community survey to find out what issues matter most to people in Briston/Holt/Cromer, etc. Would you mind filling in this paper survey when you get a minute over the next half an hour or so, and sticking it out of your letterbox so we can come round and pick it up? That way we won't have to disturb you again.'

If they say they haven't got the time immediately, I would just draw their attention to the Freepost address at the bottom of the form, and tell them they are feel free to fill in the survey at any time and send it back to us free of charge.

When you get to the end of your round, you go back to the beginning and get to engage in the highly satisfying game of 'spot the survey' (small pleasures) where you collect up the completed surveys from the letterboxes. Be aware that at least one in five people will conveniently forget to put their name or address on the survey, so have a pen to hand so you can jot down the house name or number and street. Connect can then fill in the rest later.

Towards the end of January, as the campaign got going, we stopped doing knock and drops and starting just using surveys as 'doorstep literature'. That is, when we went canvassing we had the surveys in hand, and at the end of the usual conversation about Steff, why he was running, questions about the elector's party affiliations and so on, we gave them the survey as a 'chance to explain their views in more depth' and asked them to freepost it back to us.

We got a surprising number of returns in the post by doing this, though it produced a much lower hit-rate than the knock and drops.

Because we started surveying well before Christmas, we were able to build up our awareness of local issues and a database of information before the proper campaign even got started.[31] I can't recommend this approach enough for helping to hit the ground running in the New Year. Not only had we collected a solid base of local issues on which Steff could take action (to create a 'track record' which we could reference later on in the campaign) but we also had a whole host of new contact details (namely, phones and emails) and, most importantly of all, voter IDs.

As campaigns gather momentum, they get more and more complex as new threads are added. You have volunteers to recruit, literature to deliver, doors to knock on, phone calls to make, press appearances to organise, posters to put up, fires to fight. Quite a good way to ease yourself

---

[31] To refer to one particularly brilliant survey response, there is nothing like 'CORRUPT ACTIVITIES IN PARISH COUNCIL' written in capital letters in blue felt tip pen to draw your attention to an issue...

into this quagmire, therefore, is to bite the bullet and start early, but to focus initially only on the reassuringly straightforward task of distributing and processing surveys.

Our survey form was based on a local party template. There was a box for personal details, then some local questions about traffic (speeding, parking) and highways (potholes etc). This is followed by questions on some 'bigger' issues, but over which the council still has some say, such as social care provision and the environment.

At some point on the second page, it asked people to tick a box for which party they 'usually' support. There was also a box at the bottom asking people to jot down any issues they would like to raise which had not been covered by the survey – sometimes called a 'grumble box'. This is really important, as it is ridiculous to think you will ever be able to ask every relevant question.[32]

Alongside local issue collection, a major purpose of surveys is to collect voter IDs. This

---

[32] Indeed, on one of our early surveys, we did *not* put a grumble box, and one elector highlighted their dissatisfaction with the lack of space for voicing additional concerns by writing BRING BACK FOX HUNTING across the Freepost address.

doesn't mean that you should not also knock on those people's doors and engage them in conversation at a later date. But collecting those IDs early on makes your door-knocking much more efficient, because you can target the doors most receptive to a Lib Dem candidate, or know in advance that a particular person leans towards Labour, and you therefore need to push the 'help us keep the Tories out' line.

Collecting voter IDs also helps with targeting literature later on: knowing a person's voting inclinations means you can send them the most convincing and relevant messages when you begin doing targeted leaflets in the run up to polling day.

One of the first things we did in the campaign was to take a look at the existing data we had on Connect, to see where the gaps were. Our division as a whole had not been worked seriously for a long time, so there were a lot of data gaps – plenty of places where people both old and new to the area had never been contacted at all, and others where data we did have was probably out of date.

In these cases, the surveys were also useful for filling in some of those blanks, or confirming or updating existing voter preferences in Connect. By the time we had finished the campaign, I think we had collected around 200 voter IDs through surveys alone. Beware, however, of getting overly emboldened by a high level of 'Lib Dem' responses through surveys as there is a clear selection bias in the returns: Lib Dem voters are inevitably more likely than other voters to return a survey written and delivered by the Lib Dems, so running numbers on the proportion of party affiliation revealed by your survey returns won't tell you much. What looking at our numbers *did* tell us was that, in absolute terms at least, there were quite a few previously unidentified Lib Dem voters in our division, which was encouraging.

Another word of warning: processing survey data is pretty time consuming. This is another good reason to get started early on and then decrease your emphasis on surveys as your campaign schedule gets busier.

And one final word of warning: get someone other than yourself to check over all your literature, including surveys, for mistakes or poor wording. On one – admittedly small – survey print run, we ended up asking people: Which party do you normally support? Liberal Democrat, Liberal Democrat, Labour, UKIP, Green.

To process our survey data, Steff and I used an online system called *Highrise* – an American correspondence-management programme not dissimilar from the 'Casework Manager' system used by many MP constituency offices.

My very first job as Steff's right-hand person was to manage the influx of surveys and process the relevant issues as casework. I took the paper surveys, and input all the contact information and issues into Highrise. Anything that ought to go into Connect like new contact details or opinions on specific issues like the EU, I copied over.

This was a little clunky because it meant putting data in two locations. You may be able to think of a better way, but because Connect's casework feature is really not user-friendly, we felt we needed our own programme for casework management, even if it meant operating two separate systems side by side.

Once I had input the information, I drafted a letter in Steff's name, responding to the points raised by the elector. Steff had written up some template paragraphs on basic issues such as speeding, potholes, mobile phone signal and verges (yes, verges - a hot topic in North Norfolk), which I could copy and paste into the letter draft.

As issues arose, I wrote up new template paragraphs on issues like social care, the NHS, bus services and green energy. Norman's constituency office was really helpful in this, and would provide me with text they use in Norman's correspondence on national issues. This both helped us get a sense of where we stood in relation to the national party line and also allowed us to name-drop Norman in our correspondence – always a winner.

Once I had drafted a letter, I uploaded it onto the relevant voter's profile on Highrise, so that Steff could review it, make any changes he wanted, and then print, sign, and post it. We used the same system for people who raised casework issues on the doorstep, as well as for people who contacted me or Steff by email, letter or phone about casework-related issues.

Over the course of the campaign, and in addition to leaflets, we sent well over 200 personally addressed casework letters to electors about more than fifty different issues. That means at least one in twenty voter households in our division received a personal casework letter from Steff at some point during the campaign, as well as all the other literature.

The surveys elicited some excellent – if unlikely – policy proposals[33], some innovative and slightly passive-aggressive form-filling approaches (see

---

[33] 'MORE BUSES, MORE OFTEN, MORE PLACES. 5AM TO 11PM. FREE TO EVERYONE (PAID BY THE TAXPAYER)'.

images at end of chapter), some unexpected answers (see images), and, occasionally, such unabashed and incoherent xenophobia that I had to start seriously questioning my faith in humanity.[34]

But the surveys also provided enormously valuable insight into local issues and opinions. It was the surveys that helped us build connections to local parents in Briston and Melton Constable in relation to what became perhaps the most significant event of the campaign: the saving of the lollipop lady (as discussed in Chapter 3).

The surveys also drew our attention to a number of complex pieces of individual casework, in relation to people who had been appallingly badly let down by local services and processes, and felt they had nowhere else to turn. We may never have discovered these problems, nor been able to do anything about them, were it not for the

---

[34] 'STOP IMMIGRATION TODAY. This country will lose it's identity and culture. Immigrant's are slowly taking over (Birmingham School) (The Lord Mayor of London: A Muslim) what a joke!! can you politicians not see what is happening.' This person then ticked the box indicating that they normally vote Liberal Democrat...

surveys. Steff later ran a 'bus service survey' in five of the larger villages in the division, where residents had highlighted the infrequency (read: non-existence) of the bus service.

Steff had rightly identified that the council had only ever surveyed bus *users* in its research on service provision. This meant the council never gathered information on what was stopping non-bus-users from catching the bus, and was therefore failing to gather data that could help increase demand and make a service more financially viable.

By this point in the campaign, we had already produced a great deal of targeted literature to our core voter base, but had not made a huge amount of headway on reducing the pool of No Data voters, except by gnawing slowly away at it through door-knocking. We therefore decided to only send the bus surveys to No Data voters, and to include a question about their voting habits.

We created a postcard-sized questionnaire, which was sent by Royal Mail to all relevant households, with a Freepost address on the other side, so they could send it straight back to us. Not only did the bus survey help shed light on a few more of the 'unknown' voters, it also provided another 'track record' issue for us to point to in literature and on the doorstep.

3. Regardless of price or frequency, what would make the biggest difference to your experience of using a bus?

 YES.

After the referendum on Britain's membership of the European Union, what do you think should be the top priority for the government?

☑ Getting the best deal on trade ~~even if it means allowing EU citizens to work freely in the UK~~

☑ Cutting immigration

☐ Working with other countries to protect the environment

9

Canvassing

(Steff)

Almost everyone appeared to know what canvassing meant apart from me – until October 2016, that is. I think it is because we grew up in a village that wasn't big enough for canvassers to make the trip – I now know exactly what that calculation entails – and the fact that where I later lived in Birmingham, 'canvassing' was something candidates did around pots of tea with influential, multigenerational families.

I soon understood from people's door labelling that canvassing is something some people don't want. In fact, it can be even further down the list than door-to-door sales, tax collection and white-washing-satisfaction-level enquiries.

Before I started on my own patch, I had the opportunity to go out canvassing with someone else. This was excellent, and I got to understand what it was like to be the 'other' Jehovah's Witness – the one who is clearly in training, rather than just there to bolster the friendly smiles.

The person I was with was a little peculiar in their approach. Having spent the car journey talking normally, they erupted into a Dickensian version of English as soon as they were presented with a real elector.[35]

"Excuse me, Sir, might I ask, have you considered who you will be voting for in the forthcoming by-election, and whether we can count on your vote?"

This seemed to baffle the elector as much as it did me. The candidate was answered nonchalantly and dismissed.

I was dumbfounded. Having got the poor chap out of his chair or dinner, did we not want to try and persuade him of the merits of voting for our candidate?

The language is, I think, actually quite indefensible. No wonder people think politicians live on a different planet: rosettes a-blazing, speaking like a Victorian. But perhaps that reflects the last time any canvassing training was actually done!

The purpose of my mentor was undeniable: "We only want to find out if there's a chance they

---

[35] Elector is the word given to people who are allowed to vote in an election: members of the 'electorate'.

might vote for us. If they don't seem interested, then they probably won't bother to vote at all. And there's no point trying to convince a Strong Tory or Strong Labour voter. Cut and move on to the next door."

This still feels a bit short-sighted. But in this instance, we did only have a short amount of time until the election, and only had we started earlier might it have been worth engaging the elector in conversation that could have developed their thinking about it.

In fact, as my own campaign shaped up, the canvassing style changed enormously. By the time we were into the swing of things, the canvassing script was a core element of my sequenced campaign messaging. Sometimes we were out hunting for new voters about whom we knew nothing; other times we were checking back on previous supporters to see if we had won their support, or encouraging recent confirmations to make a plan for the day to help make sure they turned out.

Planning it in this way meant there was often something more relevant and less abrupt to talk about and the question of who they were going to vote for could be dropped in at the end.

Whatever I was doing, I was adamant that it should sound natural, and be in my own words.

And when I took out groups of canvassers, I made sure I briefed them on the purpose of the session, not the specific wording they should use, so they could do the same. And although there are still those in the party who are die-hard rosette fans, I used the Liberal Democrat lanyards I'd saved up from previous party conferences to make nice 'Team Melton Constable' badges, often with the canvasser's name on if I knew they were coming.

At the heart of all this is what I mentioned in the introduction: the main focus of the campaign was to gather as much data as possible about people who might vote for me, so the closing days could be spent making sure that they actually went out to vote (not forgetting postal voters, whose ballot papers arrive several weeks earlier).

The party has many things wrong with it, but its data systems are superb. The central database, as Freya has said, is incredibly powerful if you know how to operate it. Minivan is an incredibly useful mobile version for canvassing and if I were you, I would simply ban anyone from insisting on paper canvass sheets: the additional time it takes to enter them into a machine, the chances of data being lost or out of date, and the sheer hassle, means there are better things to do with people who refuse to use technology (although I'm not sure that attitude conforms to a liberal, progressive outlook).

I tested both approaches: there are signal and battery issues with Minivan, but they are worth overcoming in the interests of getting data into the system without an extra step.

Canvassing is surprisingly compelling: a bit like a big, long strategy game. If you use Minivan, you get to see your 'score' as you go. On top of the things Freya has mentioned, here are some canvassing tips for the uninitiated:

1. Plan your loo breaks, which may involve a separate mission to find loos.

2. Give yourself little rewards – chocolates, rests, or the chance to go home, after you have spoken to five favourable people, for example.

3. Remember it is a long game – 'powering through' to get to a particular target will seem depressingly insignificant in the grand scheme of things.

4. Set realistic and achievable targets – such as knocking on a certain number of doors, which is something you can actually control and therefore achieve.

5. Don't spend all afternoon looking for one person. I was determined to find the 'other' elector registered at a particular property, so I asked the over-canvassed elderly occupant where I could find them. He gave me directions up the road, down a farm track, through some trees, to a caravan, where he said I would find his son. Indeed I did – and luckily he still seemed to be permanently resident in the house and would be able to vote for me, but by the time I found him I was actually outside the division (and down half an hour).

6. Practice your polite 'getting out of conversations' line. You may need to deploy it for party zealots more than bigots. The latter often say things to achieve the same purpose rather than out of any true belief – but the former can be fatal to an ardent campaigner's day plans.

7. Try to stick to good coffee (although beware the impact on tip (1) and stay away from sausage rolls with sell-by dates further than a year away.

10
Social media
(Steff)

This may sound strange from someone who has worked on the web for their whole career, but social media didn't have a big role to play in my campaign in Melton Constable.

The numbers of people accessing social media, and the amount of time they spend on it, may seem mind-blowing and, for mass-market communications, it is an essential ingredient in the communications mix. But as we have already talked about: the local election campaign I fought in Melton Constable was focused on activating a specific group of likely supporters with a carefully chosen set of messages to get them out to vote.

If you take the picture of mass-adoption of social media which is absolutely true at a national level, and try to apply it to that specific group of people in as tightly focused a scenario as this, it just doesn't stack up.

For a start, I doubt the adoption of social media – in particular anything beyond Facebook – is very deep in Melton Constable division.

There are several reasons for this, including the poor quality broadband and mobile phone signal, the first of which is starting to be addressed. Another is the demographic: the population is skewed towards the older end of the age spectrum, with accordingly lower uses of social media.

But the main issues are simply precision and reach. Even if you pay to target posts, the closest you can get in terms of geographic targeting is "within 20km". And there are no facilities to target organic posts. Compare this with the ability to address enveloped letters on a street-by-street basis – or to target individual households with messages that are specific to them – and it's easier to see why social media should be seen as closer to local news coverage than anything approaching targeted communications.

The reach is the other problem. If you are running your campaign through a page rather than your profile (and there are a good number of reasons you might not want to be receiving incoming casework through the same channel as you're sharing your family photos) then the proportion of followers on Facebook who will actually see each thing you post is reported to be around four per cent.

If you're starting from scratch in a new campaign, as I was, then four per cent is virtually nothing (it is four people in fact, based on the number of followers of my page at the time of writing). The main reason for this is the Facebook Edgerank algorithm: the calculation Facebook makes about which pieces of content to display on each user's newsfeed. The order of items on the newsfeed is based loosely on three functions: time decay (how recently it was posted), edgerank (which is how many likes, comments, etc, it has attracted) and affinity score (which is a function of how many other connections the page and the person following it have in common).

The third one is the biggest problem: whilst we might all have lots of connections in common with our school friends (which is why those messages about births and marriages always stick around), we are likely to have far fewer connections in common with people with whom we share a street, village or electoral division.

There is of course huge value in building up followers of a Facebook page if you are a candidate who becomes successful. I hope that, next time I stand, I can get what I post out to more than four people! It is also incredibly important to have a presence on a range of social networks in case they are the preferred means of people contacting you. I am tired of supposedly liberal colleagues having such conservative, regressive attitudes towards new forms of communications mediums that they refuse even to participate. It is as inexcusable to remove oneself from the preferred channel for under-30s to communicate (which social media is) as it is to expect everyone to do everything online and not appreciate that some people prefer – if not need – to use paper.

As a side-reference: I do not have a smart phone because I cannot stand being able to be interrupted from so many different places at all ends of the day. Messages via Facebook, What'sApp, and so on, can be impossible to log and keep track of, so I have a device that lives on my desk, through which I willingly deal with any such enquiries.

It means I am always able to enter the enquiry into my casework management system, and that I don't end up stuck to my screen when I'm not working.

When it comes to advertising on social media – the tempting opportunity to 'reach' so many thousand 'similar' people by parting with some cash, I am confident enough to be candid and say: I do not recommend spending any money on Facebook advertising for a local election campaign. This based on experience, both outside politics (where Facebook faces continued issues over the attribution of ad spend) and inside it: through an experiment we carried out to try and target the youth vote in Melton Constable. There is a section on this later in the book.

As far as my campaign went:

- I set up a Facebook page for the campaign and made use of some of Facebook's latest features like live video wherever possible – for example, at the campaign fundraiser. This was effective because it reminded my existing network outside the division of my fundraising – and helped raise a decent amount of money.
- Every time I visited a place in the division, I tried to post a picture on Twitter and Facebook (posts with pictures are four times more likely to get retweeted).
- I put my social media contact details on all literature, because of how important I think it is to meet people in the places they want to talk, whether online or in person.
- I also had a mycouncillor website, which I got for free as part of my ALDC subscription. Each time I had a story for a Focus leaflet, I published it here too. And I sent an email summary to my email list via Mailchimp at roughly the same time as I started delivering the printed Focuses.

The email address list started with the data the local party had on file and was added to through people on the site entering their email addresses but also 'scraping' contact details from the casework management system I used. There is nothing stopping you from doing this in political campaigning, as long as you make sure the relevant disclaimer is put on whatever media people are entering their contact details into.

For example: on the residents' surveys, it was part of the 'impressum' (see earlier chapter) and I even have my county council email autoresponder set to include a sentence that means anyone who contacts me via email with a piece of casework is able to be added to my Mailchimp mailing list.

Other than that, specific digital activities had very little to do with my campaign. And it doesn't seem to have hindered the outcome.

11

Design and Messaging
(Steff)

As Freya mentioned, 'Literature' means leaflets. Lots of them. And with them, the perpetual debate about how many leaflets is the right number.

This argument has always bemused me: surely what matters is whether what's in the leaflets is useful, interesting or entertaining to people, not how often they are produced?

From my exposure to party literature, I felt like we tended to write exclusively for only two of the groups in Chris' book: *Settlers* and *Pioneers*. The pioneers are the 'people like us', and they are treated with text heavy tomes about all the wonderful values of liberal democracy. The settlers are people, according to the Values Based Segmentation model, who are more concerned with their immediate surroundings: being safe, having access to the fundamental things everyone needs in life. This has resulted, in my opinion, in literature that is written like a screaming tabloid newspaper and can be patronising beyond belief.

I am paraphrasing of course, and I'm not talking about the 'looks-like-a-tabloid' newsletter that is a famous part of North Norfolk's stock – I actually get pretty good responses from people about it as a local news source. There is also a time for screaming hysteria – like the final leaflet we put out in Norman's successful re-election campaign in June this year, warning of the implications of a Tory victory.

On top of this, my beef is that both, indeed all, types of leaflet tend to focus on the "look what the Lib Dems have done". This is an important ingredient in political campaigning but it is not the only thing that affects people's thinking.

And this is just the words bit! Goodness knows how many people actually read the words. The aesthetic qualities of some of the literature the Lib Dems put out are *shocking*. It says a lot that the desktop software package the party recommends is literally the cheapest on the market, and doesn't work on Macs.

Saying 'people don't like things that are fancy' is one thing (as character Malcolm Tucker said in sitcom *The Thick of It*: "People don't like their politicians to be comfortable. They don't like you having expenses, they don't like you being paid, they rather you lived in a fucking cave.") But thinking about the way a piece of literature is designed and what that communicates is a different thing.

I decided that the way the words and pictures were arranged on the page did matter, and would influence people. And that I wanted to tell a story throughout the campaign literature that brought people to a point where they wanted to vote for me, rather than banging on about the same idea ceaselessly. I also didn't want to be photographed next to any bus stops or potholes.

So I was extremely grateful to find that Tim – our design guru mentioned earlier on – was on board, despite a long family history of supporting a different party. I tried to brief him carefully about what we wanted the design to achieve:

- Quiet, understated competence, without being flashy.
- Simple, cheap to produce design.
- Repeatable, recognisable motifs.

I also produced a simple messaging framework that would help guide the type of content to go into the leaflets. This was based on the fact that I was an unknown candidate at the start, and wanted to win first time round.

Message sequencing

Phase 1

Theme: Why I'm involved in politics

Key messages: values, vision, motives, who I am.

Call to action: sign up to the newsletter, like the Facebook page.

Phase 2

Theme: How I will do it

Key message content: contactable, local, accessible, in touch, doing *with* not 'to' or 'for' people, party funded by donations and worked by volunteers.

Call to action: come and meet me, get in touch direct, put up poster.

Phase 3

Theme: What that means in practical terms (campaigns and causes). Big vision.

Key message content: what I've done, recent campaign victories, ongoing issues, manifesto-related stuff. When communities come together there's nothing that can't be done.

Call to action: vote for me.

The first two leaflets were on plain paper, printed on the Riso in the office. The third, which was the important final one, was in full colour, glossy and folded: a demonstration of the permanence and investment in the promises I was making (although not as rock-like as Ed Milliband's 'tombstone').

As Freya has described, we went through the literature plan in advance to help manage design and print and delivery deadlines, and this three-phase approach was mainly seen in the three Focus leaflets. But the full range of places where the tone and content of the messaging framework was referred to was not limited to printed leaflets and letters. It also affected the content of press releases, what was posted on the website and even the canvassing briefings we held for people who joined us on the doors.

Politics – especially Liberal-leaning politics – appears singularly to lack appreciation for the aesthetic, which fully upholds the classifications Chris Rose was referring to. Realising that the whole of Western capitalism has grown up around the power of brands to affect people's thinking, motivation and behaviour, and investing properly in image development and design, in the broadest sense of the word, is a huge opportunity that could affect everything, from people's preferences at the ballot box, to the calibre of candidates the party can attract. If I were in charge of rebuilding the party, I would start here.

12
Coffee mornings
(Steff)

Pierre Bütikofer, the excellent district councillor for Astley Ward, has many stories about his election success in 2015. The most resonant of these is one he is easily persuaded to regale, about what happened when his Conservative opponent discovered he'd been going to Hindolveston coffee morning for weeks.

I won't steal it from him, as it will remove the pleasure the first-time listener experiences hearing it from the horse's mouth. But it led to a piece of advice Pierre was kind enough to share with me early on.

All over Norfolk, people get together in village halls on a regular basis to eat cake. This is a true fact, even though it sounds like the sort of thing American movie writers would make up. Sometimes these events are well-advertised, sometimes they are virtually masonic, but the ones I have been to have always been fun.

They are by no means a place for capital-P Politics, so if you are unable to separate yourself from your rosette, steer clear of them: nobody wants to talk about the Liberal Democrats. But they are a great way simply to meet people and find out more about the village. Newcomers be warned though: you may get asked to sit elsewhere. This is not, as I first thought, because people are wary of newcomers or knew I was a candidate: it is simply that there is a strict table plan that you have failed to observe. And by 'observe', I mean 'guess in advance'.

Some of the coffee mornings I attended were veritable institutions. Some were struggling groups of people trying to rebuild the heart of their community after losing a community asset or simply seeing huge changes in the population. You can learn a lot about a village simply by gathering with people in the nearest public space.

I was also reminded of the vital role that churches play in keeping communities together in ways that don't involve services. As an atheist Quaker who is suspicious of all organised religion, I went away from Briston Salvation Army coffee morning with a real sense of respect for them.

Amusingly, I also wasn't the only person who could have been accused of soliciting at these events: I noticed a decent bit of booking going on for the local self-employed gardener too. He rides his tools around in a child trailer on the back of his pushbike and has exactly the sort of story that makes Tories think everyone who is dealt a difficult hand should be able to 'pull themselves up and get on with it'.

He has though, and he is a credit to himself for it.

13
Fundraising
(Steff)

At some point in the process of deciding to stand for election, I realised it was going to cost me money if I was going to succeed. The human resource power of an army of volunteers is a massive help, but getting things printed, and posted when you can't find the addresses, or simply driving around campaigning, all costs money.

I would suggest that a typical local election candidate – building up towards a county campaign – needs to find about £5,000 in order to afford all the fundamental ingredients. Of course, the period immediately prior to the election itself is strictly controlled and the total that can be spent (excluding travel) cannot exceed an amount that is calculated based on the number of electors. In our case it was just under £1,200.

As Freya has mentioned, the precise definition of how eligible costs were worked out nearly caught us out.

We spent quite a lot of money doing things in

Melton Constable that were not directly to do with the campaign – things like buying a copy of the guidelines for how School Crossing Patrol sites are assessed. And it all adds up.

I have had some experience raising money for various things in the past, but never something that was quite so personal, or offered potential sponsors absolutely no prospect of a financial return (as opposed to very little prospect, which is the reality anyone looking at investing in an early stage business should assume is their chance of a return).

Interestingly, *crowd funding* is something I didn't know I was doing the first time I did it. In 2008, comedy writer Guy Browning and I asked an entire village in Oxfordshire to help make a film. Local people put up the cast and crew in their homes, the Women's Institute did the catering and the local hair salon opened at 5am to get the cast through hair and make up.

Tortoise in Love premiered in London's Leicester Square where the red carpet was flanked by tractors and watched live by five million people, before being sold around the world. And as well as acting in, producing, delivering and watching the film, the people in the village and beyond also helped get together the money to make it happen.

It wasn't until 2011 when I was invited to the MIPTV festival in Cannes to talk about the project that I realised we were an example of something that was starting to become a seriously popular way of raising money for things – helped by that stage by a number of different crowdfunding websites that were springing up to guide people through the process and make things like payments easier.

So I settled down to do some research, and decided on Crowdfunder.co.uk. They take a small percentage on top of the payment fee, which I would argue is wholly justified given the improved performance your fundraising will experience, using software that has been designed to make it super easy for people to sign up and send money.

Another bugbear of mine is the economically illiterate saying: "Ooh, we can't ask people for money and then give a percentage of it to third parties". If none of the money that is raised can be given to third parties to improve the overall chances of success of the project, then what on earth can it be spent on once it's raised?

But successful crowdfunding is not as simple as "build it and they will come". You need a compelling story. If you are thinking about using crowd funding for anything, here are my top tips for success:

1. Plan your campaign before you start: how are you going to spread the word, what PR could you use to generate reach, etc?

2. Work it 'old school', in advance to get some people to commit to decent pledges once you go live, and don't go live until you know where at least half your pledges are going to come from.

3. Set an achievable target.

4. Make the rewards really appealing but simple.[36]

5. Make a great video that paints a picture of what the world will be like when you succeed.

6. Focus on place: most people care more about their own community than they do any given cause.

7. Find and feature well-known local backers.

---

[36] For our rewards, we had things like a "Make Melton Constable Great Again" red cap for people who donated over £100, and a personal deluxe tour of the Melton Constable area for those who donated more than £1,000.

8. Have some news and announcements up your sleeve to make during the fundraising period.

Raising the money had another benefit too, in that it gave us an excuse to host an event and bring people together. I decided to hold the event in a pub in Norwich, my home city, and it attracted a pretty different set of people: some who probably wouldn't be able to help in person but who found it easy to hop on a train from London or Birmingham, and some who were just passing and fancied finding out a bit more about the bizarre decision I had taken to change my professional direction.

The event, which was organised by two friends in Norwich, was terrific fun. It gave us the chance to take some achingly trendy pictures of politics, the likes of which rarely grace Focus leaflets, and also to live-stream the whole thing on Facebook. And the entry to the bar even said: "Ballroom Closed, Comedy Night", which is as reasonable a description for a Liberal Democrat fundraiser as you could wish for.

At the time, and probably still at the time of writing, Facebook was heavily promoting *Facebook Live,* meaning that live videos were getting extra prominence on people's news feeds. All sorts of other people joined in through this medium. Here are some of the valuable comments that went on in the comments section of the Facebook live feed:

Mary: Hi Steff!
Paul: red wine please
Karen: Hey Felix!
Cath: Luv that guy-Felix! Oh and you too Steff
Nico: Catching up on this - EPIC
Ed: Yaaaaaay
Dave: forgive me for not being there despite saying I would be. See you tomorrow for delivery and coffee in Briston!
Ed: Who are the two people in front of the camera, are they Secret Service?
Bethany: Hiiiiiii from Kenya. The lions all have their 3D glasses on.
Graham: Bring it on SA. Gerrroooovy shirt.
Freya: nice chin. Says Sue.
Luzie: Fab
Ed: are those the white balloons of freedom?
Neil: Steff for leader of the universe
Ed: well done steff! rousing stuff X
Ed: DAAAVE
Lesley: Mine's a Pinot Grigio...
Lesley: Well said, Steff! x
Kat: Hello!
Neil: Get that beardo out of the way

Neil: Go Steff!

Lesley: Break a leg, Steff! x

Abby: We're very proud!

William: Anticipation building...

Abby: Whoop! Hello from Birmingham

William: We're here. Go Steff

Aidan: Nailed it Steff!

Aidan: Hi Neil!

Mary: Hi steffan

Graham: Trump cap

Lesley: Here in Florida, we've just had the daily Press Briefing from Trumpworld. You made a lot more sense.

William: Steffan Aquarone - yes we can.....

Marcus: Nice work man

Neil: Well said Steff

Neil: Hi leavers

Neil: Hi Dave

Neil: Go steff!

Ashley: Steff for PM!

Neil: Soz

Neil: Don't end it!

Neil: Not snarky! We love you!!

Neil: *Lavvers! Ffs

Marcus: Nice work Steff... Good luck!

Neil: Go steff! I BELIEVE

This might all seem frivolous, but the live stream

got more than 700 views on the night which was, well, a lot more than the people in the room. And the campaign raised a total of more than £2,700.

Raising the money wasn't all plain sailing though. Another successful milestone in the campaign, another complaint made to the returning officer. This time, their letter said:

"The complaint refers to your use of the crowdfunder.co.uk website to raise funds for your election campaign. I would remind you that the Electoral Commission has issued guidance for candidates and agents for the 2017 local elections – Part 3 of which relates to Spending and Donations and it is important that you comply with these regulations. In particular, there is clear guidance issued in respect of donations with value of over £50 and the complaint made to me is that there are a number of donations detailed on your crowdfunder web page of a value of £100 or more, including a single donation of £1,000. I advise that it is for you and your agent to satisfy yourselves as to whether these donations can be accepted to support your campaign expenditure under the terms of the Electoral Commission guidance and that it will be necessary for you and your agent to sign a declaration in this regard."

Great, well, that was perfectly reasonable. And we were perfectly compliant. You know what they say: you're not doing it right if no one is complaining about it.

14
Leaflets and volunteer networks
(Freya)

It is a truth universally acknowledged that, if you have not been chased by at least one mad dog, and still have skin left on your knuckles, then you are probably not doing enough delivering.[37]

---

[37] Really hardcore deliverers I know carry spatulas as weapons and can leap six feet into the air from a standing start to scale any perimeter fence or wall in the face of oncoming canine fury. This is dandy, unless the dog can also jump. During the campaign, I was delivering in a village when a dog leapt over a high garden wall and ran at me. The owner rushed out of the house and yelled '*stay very still!*' which is probably the most effective way to make a person want to flee for their life. Spatula-less, I had no choice but to stand and pray. Thankfully, the dog lost interest and ran off down the road, at which point the owner, pulling on their shoes to go after him, told me exasperatedly that the

In all seriousness, leaflets are the bedrock of a successful campaign. New campaigners (including me) tend to start out dubious about this. Doesn't all that party political rubbish just end up straight in the recycling, or on the floor, people ask?

In their book *101 Ways to Win an Election,* Ed Maxfield and Mark Pack explain why you need masses of leaflets to even begin making an impact, and the book is essential reading for any campaigner, seasoned or new.

Delivery is a funny business. If you do enough of it, you will find you have conditioned yourself to have strong emotional reactions to different types of letterbox. To this day, when I pass buildings with external letterboxes attached to their gates or fences, I feel a rush of affection for the householders. By contrast, however ecologically aware you consider yourself to be, you will learn to hate draft excluders with a passion.

During the campaign, I had more bizarre encounters while delivering during the campaign than I can count on two hands.

Some low points include driving down a long, winding, extremely muddy lane for a good fifteen minutes (in the hope of reaching an elusive

_____

dog had 'never done that before'.

dwelling at the end, indicated on the map), getting stuck halfway along in a muddy quagmire, extracting the car with some effort (and a lot of muddy wheel-spray), only to discover that the house, once we finally located it, was surrounded by an eight-foot razor-wire, with no letterbox in sight, and giant red signs everywhere reading BEWARE OF THE DOG.

Another gem was when Steff received a voicemail, just as we finished a lengthy delivery round, from a woman who screeched for five minutes down the phone, beginning with "when you see a sign saying *do not deliver* it MEANS do not deliver! My dog goes bananas every time something is put through the letterbox".

She ended with: "I'll hold you responsible if the dog has a bloody fit tonight!"

Because the woman did not leave her name or address, and called from a withheld number, it was anyone's guess which house was actually hers; Steff and I have been back to deliver and canvass in that village many times, and never have either of us found a 'do not deliver' sign on any door. In the end I had to assume that the lady in question lived in the house that had stuck a 'No Cold Calling' sign a few inches above the letterbox.

I was sorely tempted to deliver her a written definition of 'cold-calling' to help clarify the problem. A friend from the local office had a better suggestion: given that the answer to this woman's woes would surely be to fit an external letterbox on her gate, she suggested we post her a suitable mail order catalogue.[38]

Things can also go wrong well before you even start delivering. For our very first proper action day (see chapter 15 for more on action days), Steff and Tim had slaved away to write and design our second Focus leaflet in time to get it printed on the Riso at the office before the big event.

Unfortunately, the day before, something had gone horribly wrong in the printing: the orangey-red colouring of the header had bled down onto the word 'FOCUS', making the top of the front page look like the scene of a massacre. Having decided that the leaflets were not deliverable in this state, Steff hurriedly got on the phone to Roger of Century Printing and asked if he just might be able to print a couple of thousand at short notice.

This, predictably, cost more than the Riso.[39] It

---

[38] I often wish we had the guts to actually do this...

[39] That is why you should always have contingency funds planned into your budget. It is inevitable that, at some stage of the campaign, you will need to buy your

also meant that our poor mother had to drive to Stalham at 8am the next morning, to get the leaflets as soon as the printers opened, and get them to Briston in time for the start of the action day, so that we didn't end up with a load of volunteers and nothing to deliver.

Despite my excellent driving-time guesswork displayed earlier on, I have an infamously terrible understanding of geography. So when I lightly asked my mum whether we could just "pop to Stalham on the way to Briston tomorrow morning", she couldn't resist drawing me a map of exactly how *not* 'on the way' Stalham is to Briston (see picture below).

It is worth pausing here to talk a bit more about our Mum and her partner Bill, who played an indispensable role in the campaign by being what they refer to as 'the backstops'. This basically meant that, although they did not commit to things like regular delivery or door-knocking, when things went wrong (which they regularly did) they were there to fly in and save the day.[40]

On one particularly memorable occasion, Steff

---

way out of a crisis.

[40] Bill, in particular, did a huge amount of short-notice delivering in the more obscurely located villages.

and I learned the hard way that babies and campaigning do not mix. Jill was bed-bound with flu and that week's schedule was so tight, we couldn't afford to lose a day. Filled with idyllic images of Steff knocking on doors with Felix smiling endearingly from a baby-carrier (surely a vote-winning combination), we drove off to the back of beyond. Felix, however, decided he did not care for Baconsthorpe and told us in no uncertain terms just as we got out of the car.

Four doors later, with Steff trying to explain his views on local recycling provision over Felix's screams, we rang my Mum, who agreed to cancel all her plans and come meet us in a pub in Briston to relieve us of our charge.

If you can find someone to be your backstop, you might actually make it through the campaign with all your marbles.

In case you are now thoroughly put off by the horror stories above, delivery entails all sorts of lovely experiences as well. For instance, on one cold February morning (bear with me), I cycled to Itteringham to do a delivery round, and as I reached one of the last houses – pretty knackered and chilled to the bone – the door opened and the best puppy I have ever seen came scrambling into the front garden.

The dog's very amiable owner let me hold it

while I explained why I was there, and I left to finish up the round with puppy-inspired zeal.

I even had a brief encounter with a member of the House of Lords. Mannington Hall and its estate are part of Steff's patch, and its owners are the lovely Lord and Lady Walpole. I was out delivering with Bill, and this was back in the days when we were still trying to find every house on the map (and would therefore spend 45 minutes looking for three houses rather than deciding that 45 minutes of saved time was probably worth £1.50 in stamps).

We went up the grand driveway to Mannington Hall, and parked beside the bridge leading over the moat (yes, the moat). The front door did not have a letterbox and a quick look around each corner of the house revealed no obvious place for post. Bill is a lot bolder than me when it comes to striding up to people's front doors (I am pretty timid, especially when I can't make sure the garden is angry-dog-free, or when there is any intimation that the householder might shout at me.[41])

So while I skulked around, voicing concerns

---

[41] This has never actually happened to me while delivering.

about trespassing, Bill just went up to the imposing front door and hammered on it, at which point a rather surprised Lady Walpole opened the door, and Bill brightly informed her that Steff was running for the council, and that she might remember him from when he organised a music concert in her back garden fifteen years ago, and that he was a 'special' young man who really deserved her vote. I wasn't sure whether to run away in horrified embarrassment or laugh out loud.

All these delights aside, delivery is time- and energy-consuming. The most important thing you can do early on in your campaign, therefore, is try to shift some of the burden off your own shoulders and onto unsuspecting victi-....volunteers.

In chapter 7, I listed the pieces of literature Steff and I aimed to produce over the campaign. I also noted that we would never have been able to deliver it all just between the two of us. We reckon we hand-delivered around 25,000 individual pieces of campaign literature between December and May. In a densely popular area, such as parts of Briston, you can get fifty leaflets out in about half an hour (that allows just over thirty seconds per leaflet).

In some of our more scattered villages, such as Itteringham, fifty leaflets takes more like an hour and a half. Let's say that, on average, delivering fifty leaflets takes an hour. That means, even if we don't account for travel between villages, delivering 25,000 leaflets would take around 500 hours. If an average working week is 35 hours, it would take one person working full time for well over three months to deliver all that literature.

You get the idea. Forgive the melodrama, but you *need to get some help*.

Getting started is the tricky part.
One way to kick things off is to use Connect to search for people in your patch who have previously done delivery for the party. They should be marked by the 'deliverer' tag. This will pull up the list of people most likely to help you. But don't make assumptions – more often than not, people end up delivering because they know or like the specific candidate in question, rather than out of fierce party loyalty. There is no guarantee that just because Mr Singh delivered for the candidate in your area back in 2013, he will have any interest in doing so for you.

When you have your list of former deliverers, it is good to run it past an old hand from your local party office. This will give you important scraps of info and avoid foot-in-mouth situations. Sometimes, people have explicitly told the party that they are no longer able to deliver (for instance, they are caring full time for a family member, or have become disabled) but their deliverer tag has not been removed from Connect.

Save yourself from being on the end of someone's justifiable wrath about being called for the umpteenth time about volunteering, and check that the list is up to date. When I ran the list past Ed Maxfield he gave me multiple useful tips such as: be sure to mention to that person that you are a friend of Norman Lamb, as they normally only help Norman rather than local candidates.

And: the woman in that couple can be a little brusque on the phone. She will probably say no to whatever you ask but then you'll get a call back three minutes later from her husband saying they will help.

And: that David Thomas is *Dave,* as in the Dave you have met multiple times. So don't call him Mr Thomas on the phone or he'll laugh at you. It is particularly helpful being able to name-drop mutual friends. If one deliverer is specifically an old friend of Ed's, then rather than saying that you are calling on behalf of the North Norfolk Lib Dems or whatever, it might be best to say that Ed suggested you get in touch.

We got about five regular volunteers just by

calling round the – admittedly short – list of former deliverers. They also turned out to be some of our most reliable helpers.

Our next port of call for building a volunteer network was the 'Members and Supporters list' for our patch. This is a list kept by the local office of all party members as well as people who – though not actual party members – are keen supporters of the party's work locally. Some of these people are also tagged as deliverers in Connect, so we removed those to avoid duplication, and then once again asked someone for any relevant information.

Quite a few people on that list were known to be too elderly or busy to help. Some of them were just rather out of date (for example, one of them had in fact recently become a Conservative district councillor!).

Steff managed to scoop up quite a few deliverers just by asking on the doorstep or at local events. The candidate is always much more likely to get help this way, but it is still worth asking if you are out and about on their behalf. If someone on the doorstep seems enthusiastic about the candidate, emphasise to them that they won't be able to win without some help, and that even half an hour delivering leaflets on their street would be an enormous help.

The key thing is to ask. The worst that can happen is that someone politely turns you down.

By the end of the campaign, Steff and I had 25 deliverers on our 'volunteers list'.[42] Few of them delivered a round for every single leaflet instalment, but they all worked incredibly hard and we owe our election success in no small part to them. You need to have more deliverers than you think is necessary, because one or two people will always be unavailable.

I remember one particularly ill-fated week in which Steff was away for 48 hours on a business trip, and on ringing round our deliverers I discovered that one had just had a hip operation, another was bed-bound with a nasty virus, a third had tripped over a puppy and broken their ankle and a fourth had just moved into a new house, only to discover that there was no electricity or water. Having extra people to fall back on was, therefore, crucial.

On another occasion, Steff and I discovered that we had misunderstood the rules regarding the election spending period about four days

---

[42] But the list of people who had helped us in some way during the campaign ran to well over 60 people, excluding donors.

before the cut-off date.[43] We had thought that, if a leaflet run was *printed* by the cut-off date, but delivered *after* it, then its production cost would not count towards our budget. In fact, a leaflet needs to be *on a doormat* before the cut-off for it not to count in the spending.

This meant all our well-laid plans for the next four days were suddenly moot. I had to call round every deliverer on the list – as well as plenty of coercible friends and family – and beg them to help us at short notice. Having plenty of foot soldiers on hand was the only way we got through those four hectic days.

You need to keep volunteers sweet. It is far too easy to start taking people for granted, especially when they are generous with their time and don't complain loudly enough when you are over-burdening them. In particular, it is key not to exhaust your deliverers, or they will do the first two rounds and then disappear off the face of the earth.

Especially if you have older people helping you, then you need to bear in mind their energy-levels. Ringing up that lovely couple in their late eighties

---

43 I can' emphasise this enough: *make sure you understand the rules on the election spending period!*

to ask them to deliver yet another bundle, when they just finished the last one yesterday morning, is probably not wise.

It is good to keep in touch with your deliverers, and thank them each time for what they have done, no matter how small. I got into the habit of contacting all our volunteers about a week after they had received their bundles, just to check in on how they had found the delivery, whether there had been any problems, whether there were any houses they had struggled to find, what the response had been like.

By framing these moments of contact as a 'checking in' rather than a 'checking up on' exercise (I always made it clear that it was fine if they hadn't yet completed the round, that I was just trying to keep up with what had and had not been delivered), they became a good way to form relationships with our volunteers. A few people communicated with me by text or email, whereas others were only contactable by phone – it soon became clear what were people's preferred means of communication, and I took the lead from them.

One of our deliverers and I ended up in an ongoing email exchange, in which – at the end of every leaflet round – she would send a tongue-in-cheek email from the perspective of her dog (called MossDog, her loyal delivery 'helper'), complaining about being taken for granted, with an accompanying photo showing him exhausted in a different location in her house or garden.[44]

If you are nice to your deliverers, they will go the extra mile. One deliverer had been volunteering for the party for years, but was married to a woman who preferred to keep out of politics. I often liaised with her by email or on the phone about dropping off leaflet bundles to her husband. She was always perfectly friendly, but we never asked her or pushed her to deliver for us, sensing her lack of enthusiasm.

Yet, towards the end of the campaign, when her husband was unexpectedly unavailable to help, she offered to do the round herself. Her husband emailed us a few days later apologising for having been unavailable, and telling us in stunned tones that it was first time his wife had ever volunteered to help a candidate.

Once you have formed the beginnings of a

---

[44] Email received, 24 April 2017: "I've delivered all the leaflets and I'm cold and wet and am going to ring Puppy Line to report that Aquarone guy. People are very nice about him on my round, but I've sorted that. Now going to get warm and think about being a UKIP dog."

network of volunteers, you need to get them started on their first delivery bundle. Some of the people you have on board may be old hands, others may be brand new. Especially if someone is new to the game, it is important not to just drop off a box of literature and leave them to it.

Steff and I made a point of finding a time to drop all first bundles off in person, so we could introduce ourselves and explain why Steff was standing. Steff also has a bit of a bugbear – which I now share – about candidates failing to bother explaining to their volunteers the significance of what they are delivering.

Every time we printed a new leaflet, therefore, we gave a justification for it and its contents to our deliverers: for example, this leaflet is basically about setting the scene, explaining who Steff is, why he is going into politics, how he was inspired by Norman Lamb, and so on. Or: this leaflet is about discussing some of the local issues Steff has been involved in, so that people understand he is already out and about making a difference in the community. Or: this envelope contains postal voter registration forms. It may seem like a lot of effort, but the important thing about postal votes is....

It is also worth trying to suss out early on how much delivery a person is willing to do and where they prefer to do it. Some of our volunteers took on a specific village, and delivered every leaflet to that village throughout the campaign. Others were more sporadic, and were available to do a couple of deliveries in March, say, but were busy with work in April.

Some people like to do the same round over and over again, others like a change of scene. Some people prefer to deliver in their own village, others prefer the opposite. Some people are willing to drive for miles, others only have bicycles or just want somewhere close to home.

Each time a new leaflet was produced, I made a fresh list of every village in the division and crossed off the villages which were accounted for by 'regular' deliverers, so that I could see what was left over. This changed with every new leaflet, as new people joined our volunteer network and others became unavailable. Sometimes, Steff and I were able to deliver a particular village at the same time as canvassing it, taking that village out of the equation.

A map should be provided alongside all delivery bundles. Not everyone has a smartphone or access to Google maps, so it is important that this map is clear and legible. Connect has a feature which can print 'walks' for different rounds, where the households are indicated by red dots. Nonetheless, you need to bear in mind that some places are just impossible to find.

To this day there is an entire close in Briston that I swear does not exist. I have scoured Google Maps, and even asked local residents, but to no avail. Presumably the postman has special powers. We got into the habit, as we got to know the division, of circling the red dots on the maps which we knew were hard to find or were especially far out, and telling our deliverers not to spend time trying to deliver them, as we could just stick them in the post.[45]

When you come across someone who is unable, for whatever reason, to go out and deliver, it might be worth asking them whether they would be willing to hand-write or stuff envelopes. As I learned the hard way, hand-writing addresses takes an extraordinary amount of time.[46] So does manually stuffing 1,500 envelopes.

---

[45] Which reminds me: if you are going to deliver these 'outliers' by Royal Mail, don't forget to account for that in your budget - stamps cost rather a lot, so it is worth being strategic and prioritising addressed mail over generic leaflets.

[46] Especially when the lengthiest thing you have hand-written in the last year is your shopping list.

At one stage in the campaign, Steff and I decided to send postal vote registration forms to all *probs* and *defs* in the division, as well as the squeeze voters. We made the wildly optimistic assumption that we could do three per minute, and that, therefore, with three of us on the job, we could get all 1,500 done in two and a half hours. As it turned out, 'stuffing' is a dangerously misleading term. The real task is much more convoluted.

We had a stack of 1,500 personally addressed letters, that had to be matched up to an equivalent stack of postal voter registration forms, mail-merged with the elector's name and address (to make it easier for them to fill out the form). Each household had one letter, but some households contained more than one elector. So the correct number of forms had to be matched up to the letter, folded together, and then placed in an envelope, into with a *further* envelope was then placed (having had a label with our Freepost address stuck to the front) before, finally, the whole thing was sealed by running a wet sponge along the glue-strip.[47]

---

[47] This sounds a bit unnecessary until you try licking more than ten glue-strips in a row and end up

We had to set up a kind of intensive production line, and it took us the best part of two days. I managed to wear away the skin on my forefingers from repeatedly running them along the edges of folded paper. So, you see, campaign literature can be extremely hazardous.

dehydrated and with mild chemical poisoning.

X.
Briston

X
home

X
Stalham

146

15
Action Days
(Freya)

When I was thinking about how pithily to define *action days*, all I could come up with was 'days of action', which isn't especially enlightening. So a clunkier description might help: action days are when you invite lots of people – anybody you can think of who might turn up, basically – to come and help you campaign for a few hours in exchange for a free lunch. Usually there is a variety of thrilling activities on offer, from envelope stuffing and coffee-making, to door-knocking and delivery.

In early December, we ran our first action day out of the back of Steff's Lib-Dem-propaganda-adorned Volvo. He heated a proper Bialetti stove-top coffee maker on a portable gas stove. And we had chocolate biscuits. But when we were invited to another candidate's action day a few week's later, and they provided homemade soup and rolls in an actual house (rather than leaving everyone to die of exposure in a car park), we realised we probably needed to up our stakes a little.

Luckily, our first action day took place before we had any new volunteers, so the only people who came were long-suffering family members and Lib Dem stalwarts.

By the time we held our second action day in early March, standards had improved to the dizzying heights of hiring a village hall. We sent out invitations by phone and email to the members and supporters list, our existing volunteer database, and any friends, family and candidates we could think of. We also made a Facebook event for good measure. In the end, excluding Steff, myself, and our family members, about fifteen people showed up, a third of whom we had never met before.

We held the action day in Briston – the biggest of our division's villages – and, unsurprisingly, many of the new people who came were local to Briston. This highlights a significant point: holding an action day in your patch's most densely-populated or central location maximises the chances that latent supporters will come out of the woodwork, because it is much more likely they will live nearby.

Action days are a great way to meet and recruit new stoic volunteers. All of the new people who showed up to our March action day turned out to be bastions of support right through to the end of the campaign. This goes back to what I said in Chapter 6 about the value of the training sessions: coming to an event where you can be part of a group endeavour, and make connections with people over a cup of coffee or lunch, is so much more likely to motivate you than a single phone call from the candidate (however charismatic they may be), followed by delivering alone in the rain.

I will not lie to you: it did help that our action day was blessed by sunshine and that we promised everybody that Norman would be there (which he was - that wasn't just a devious ploy). Nonetheless, I really was astounded by how much everyone seemed to be enjoying themselves. Possibly we Norfolk folk are just easily pleased – give us a free tote bag and a hotdog and we'll go with you to the ends of the earth. But I think it was a lot more than that: although what we were all doing was relatively menial – mostly putting things in letterboxes – a palpable sense of purpose built up over the course of the day.

I really felt, for the first time, that what we were fighting for mattered. And seeing so many people around the room, giving up their time for Steff and saying how glad they were to be involved, was exactly the motivation we needed.

So action days are not *just* about getting a load

of literature out in one go in a relatively painless way, or about recruiting new volunteers. They are also about providing an extra morale-boost for the candidate and their campaign team, who do need an occasional reminder that all the blood, sweat and tears are worth it.

When, at the end of the day, those of us still hanging about trooped off to the pub and collapsed over a pint, I announced that we had spoken to 400 voters and delivered 2,000 leaflets that day alone. I think there was a huge feeling of collective achievement all round.

Action days take many forms, but there are a few things worth bearing in mind:

- The candidate needs to be out and about on doors as much as possible, so you need someone to act as 'front of house' in the venue you are using as base camp. In fact, it is worth having two people share this role. One of those people – in this case it was me – needs to know the area well enough to be able to hand out delivery bundles to people and point them in the right direction, and they need to be sufficiently familiar with campaigning to answer people's questions about delivery (like, what do I do if I can't find the letterbox?) and to brief door-knockers, some of whom may be doing it for the first time. This person is, in other words, in charge of tasks and logistics. The other person, by contrast, can be on hand to welcome people, provide hot drinks, make sure no one is standing alone in a corner looking lost, and be generally friendly. Our mother took on this role. Having two people at base camp meant that when I was trying to read out the wifi code to a volunteer, while giving directions to Hall Street to another, and simultaneously trying to find my mobile under reams of paper, Mum was on hand to put the kettle on for the four volunteers who had just shown up unexpectedly.

- Have a variety of tasks on offer, but not too many, as it just gets chaotic if there are loads of things going on at once. At our action day, we had leaflet delivery and door-knocking as the main priorities, and then folding and stuffing letters for anyone who was less mobile (and also as a back-up in case of bad weather). Be sure to prepare more than you think you can actually achieve in a day, as it is frustrating if – having gone to all the effort of organising an action day – you run out of tasks at 2pm.

- With the leaflets: bundle them up, attach printed maps and – if necessary – figure out where the rounds are in relation to base camp *before* the start of the action day. When everyone shows up, you'll be rushed off your feet. Anything you can do in advance to save time is worth doing.

- Advertise at the start of the day what time lunch will be, so people have the chance to gather all together for a break. Ideally this also provides the candidate with an opportunity to do a short but rousing thank-you speech.

- Talking of lunch, make sure you cater to varying dietary requirements – at least provide a vegetarian option at lunchtime and some dairy-free milk for hot drinks or fruit or herbal teas.[48] It is also worth asking on the invitations that anyone with complex dietary requirements tells you in advance.

- Have a laptop on hand, preferably with wifi access. It is always surprising what you need to look up at the last minute. Also have plenty of pens, clipboards, scrap paper, bags (to use for delivery), and spare umbrellas. One thing I would also do is print out a kind of 'cheat sheet' of key information (for an example, an explanation of the red dots on the Connect delivery maps – they indicate the location of dwellings – or a basic script for first-time door-knockers) as well as contact phone numbers for whoever is acting as

---

[48] I was surprised by how often I got requests for fruit and herbal teas. Perhaps it's a Lib Dem thing.

front-of-house.

- Finally, I think it's good, if possible, to create a mild sense of novelty. Village halls are not always the most inspiring of locations and jazzing things up a bit really helps morale, especially if the weather isn't on your side. Something as simple as a bunch of balloons will do it.[49] Or a plate of cake and some good music can make an incommensurate difference to a beige room.

---

[49] After a joint county and general election action day in another's candidate's division in late April, I ended up with eight yellow helium balloons that no one else wanted to take home. Popping helium balloons seems somehow sacrilegious, so I took them with me to meet Steff for an afternoon door-knocking session in Melton Constable. Having paraded them through the middle of the village (and received some supportive heckling from passing cars) we decided that the balloons might be a little weird on the doorsteps. So Steff and I offered them to two artisan bakers selling bread outside the butcher's shop. This prompted a lengthy discussion about where best to tie them for maximum visibility and I think we might even have scooped up two new votes.

16

Parish councils

(Steff)

I don't think I had a clue what a parish council was when I started, but I soon learned that in rural England they are the last bastion of absolute power.

There are a total of 22 parishes in Melton Constable and each of them is unique in its composition, procedure and door policy. I mention door policy in particular because, before I attended one parish council for the first time, I learned that on a previous occasion they had carried out a member of the public while he was still sitting in his chair. Given that I had also learned that some parish council chairpeople were very particular about the public only speaking in a certain section of the meeting, I thought I would go along purely out of curiosity.

In reality, whilst some parish council business involves debating passionately about the appropriate locations of dog poo bins, some parish councils have to contend with an enormous amount of challenging business. They are statutory consultees on planning applications, they collect tax from local residents which has to be prioritised to meet local needs, they are often responsible for putting together funding bids of many tens of thousands of pounds to help navigate the nightmarish complexity of modern social funding to provide facilities for the local community. And they do it all for free.[50]

They really are an essential ingredient in the political fabric, even though sometimes they can find themselves presiding over a breakaway movement within a village that would impress an experienced Basque separatist.

I found going to parish council meetings as a member of the public during the campaign to be a useful way of finding out about local issues and it was at parish council meetings that I met my two main opponents: the UKIP incumbent and the Conservative candidate.

Long before I decided to stand, I had started going along to parish council meetings to talk

---

[50] The clerks, who have some legal responsibility and are required to deal with all correspondence and minutes, are paid a nominal amount and sometimes bring their experience to more than one parish council in the same area.

about the mobile phone signal campaign – the project I had persuaded the Lib Dems to explore months before the campaign started - and I was starting to tell some local parish councils about it in areas where there was a poor signal.

But accusations soon arose about my reasons for attending, and even the motives behind the mobile phone signal campaign itself. This was frustrating as it meant this important local issue really had to take a back seat during my campaign. On one occasion, a Conservative MP, hearing of my planned attendance at a particular meeting, deluged the clerk with irrelevant information about parliamentary convention and I was actually asked not to go.

Barred from a parish council meeting! At least I didn't get carried out on my chair...

17
Your competitors
(Steff)

The best advice I can give about how to handle other candidates in an election is simply to ignore them. Unless there is a really strong 'negative' story that's worth running (for example: the Conservatives fielding a London-based candidate against Norman in the general election in 2017) it is simply not worth the time to do anything else.

Ask yourself: what possible good can come of this? If you respond, the electorate will simply see you as part of the argument. And even if you won the argument, who cares? Your opponents are never going to vote for you, after all.

The key is to have someone who will sympathise with this and allow you to vent about how so-and-so is behaving like a complete tosser, and someone else quietly to remind you that the best reaction is no reaction. I was fortunate to have people to fill both these roles.

It felt like each time we went out campaigning about a particular issue, someone would try to undermine us. Not because they were opposed to lollipop ladies, or buses or mobile phones, but presumably because they could not stand the fact we were actually campaigning.

It is hard to ignore being libelled by opposition letters in the press. This will probably happen to you, and it is only worth even considering dealing with if it is during the pre-election restricted period, when the Representation of the People Act makes it much easier to collect a campaign budget's worth of damages.

If you are unlucky you will also experience, as we did, hypocrisy, slander, loudhailers on cars, public accusations of 'fake news', and refusing to have your hand shaken after the result is announced.

Rather than reply, we just carried on doing things that made a difference – like the lollipop lady campaign – that got coverage because they were newsworthy. But we had nothing to do with one particular piece of newsworthy coverage just before the election campaign, which Freya talks about in the next chapter - however tempting it might be to assume it was a PR-generating act of self sacrifice.

18

Signboard sagas

(Freya)

Signboards can be a source of bitter neighbourly disputes. On at least two occasions, we had to deal with objections from neighbours about a sign being attached to a shared fence (even when the sign was on the side of the fence belonging to our supporter). In one case, *both* neighbours in question were actually our supporters, but happened to be engaged in an ongoing feud about land boundaries. The placement of the signboard became a kind of physical manifestation of their disagreement over property rights. So you see: never underestimate the symbolic power of party political propaganda on a stick.

A signboard is not going to instantly change the political persuasion of a blue-blooded Tory who happens to be strolling by. But signboards serve two other important purposes:

1. They help persuade the undecided that yours is the winning candidate. There is robust evidence that a large proportion of so-called 'floating

voters' simply like to back a winner. If, therefore, you can make sure that your signboards obviously outnumber those of your opponents, an undecided voter – seeing the popularity of your candidate displayed all over windows and hedgerows – is more likely to jump on the bandwagon.

2. They help reassure your supporter base – those who are already likely to vote for you – that you really are worth turning up to the polling station for because you are a) serious about winning and b) have managed to drum up a groundswell of support.

Having advertised your popularity all over the place, you do then have to push the message hard on polling week that the race is still going to be a close one, that you still need every vote you can get, and that people must therefore *still turn up to vote* rather than assume you are going to win by default.

Steff and I had a particularly exciting time with signboards. But before I get on to the riveting tale of The Great Signboard Robbery, a quick word on logistics. It turns that – as with so many aspects of campaigning – putting a hundred stakes in the ground is a lot more complicated than appears at first glance. We ended following the roughly outlined stages below: [51]

1. Begin asking voters whether they are willing to have a poster.

---

[51] Funnily enough, figuring out signboard logistics was one of the few times during the campaign that Steff and I came close to an actual argument. There are myriad ways to approach the challenge, and we had mildly contrasting beliefs about how it should be done. In the end I said: "Look, given that this falls clearly within my remit, why don't you just let me handle it?" Fortunately, Steff agreed. Especially towards the end of the campaign, candidates often start to feel like the task they have taken on is totally insurmountable and that any semblance of control over events is slipping from their fingers. It is therefore perfectly natural for your candidate to want to micro-manage, especially if they are – like Steff – actually very experienced at project-management. But the whole point of having a campaign manager is to relieve the candidate of the stress of thinking about stuff like signboard logistics, allowing them to focus largely on the task of talking to voters. That doesn't mean you shouldn't communicate or get their input. It just means that you are totally entitled to tell them to back off when they start mission-creeping all over your beautiful spreadsheets for no good reason.

a. In the earlier stages of the campaign, from January until around the end of March, we asked on surveys, doorsteps and phones whether people would be happy to have a signboard 'closer to polling day'. Then, in early April, we sent a letter to those who agreed saying that our records showed they were willing to have a signboard, and asking them to let us know if this was *no longer the case*.

b. In the later stages of the campaign, from late March onwards, we asked people if they would be willing to have a signboard and, if they said yes, explained that someone would be over within the following fortnight to put it up. And if the timings were so close, we didn't bother to confirm.

2. Make a list of all new poster sites and confirm if necessary (as per 1a above).

3. Make a list of all historical poster sites.

Connect should have a record of anyone who has agreed to have a signboard in the past

4. Remove from the historical site list anyone you have already asked so far in the campaign.

5. Contact all remaining historical poster

sites by phone asking if they will have a board again.

As with delivery volunteers, it is important not to make assumptions that people will be willing. It is possible that their name has been incorrectly recorded in Connect, that they have changed their party-political affiliation since the last election, or that – for whatever reason – they just don't want a signboard this time round. Also, unless you specifically filter the list, Connect doesn't differentiate between households that had a signboard in previous *local* elections and those who had one for a *general* election. In North Norfolk there are lots of people who support Norman Lamb but who do not support the Lib Dems in the district or county elections, which means we have to be especially careful about making assumptions. I suspect the same may be true in other constituencies with a Lib Dem MP.

6. Write to all historical poster sites for which you do not have a phone number.

For some reason, a handful of former poster sites did not have a contact number listed. Steff and I decided to send a similar letter to these people as we sent to those we had explicitly asked earlier in the campaign. That is, we sent them a letter saying that our records indicated that they had had a signboard in the past and that, unless we heard from them, we would be round to put one up in a couple of weeks' time. About a third of the households that received this letter contacted us and asked – quite politely – for us not to put up a board. Only on two occasions did we have someone contact us after we had already put up a board and ask us to take it down. So I think, all in all, it was a good time-saving strategy.

7. Combine all confirmed poster sites to form the MASTER LIST.

8. Send request to local office for however many boards you need.

9. Put up signboards

People are more willing to say 'yes' to having a signboard once they see that their neighbours have got one. Some people even began contacting us without being prompted. To deal with this snowball effect, Steff made the suggestion that we put up the signboards in two 'waves'.[52] That is, once we had a Master List of around fifty

---

[52] And this suggestion I did accept!

confirmed sites, we would put them all up in one go. Any requests that came after that initial fifty would be added to a second list, which we would allow to build up to fifty again before, as previously, putting them all up in one go.

This meant we did not need to worry about using up precious canvassing time installing random signboards in dribs and drabs, but rather allocated a day or two in the schedule entirely dedicated to putting up signboards.

The only time this system fell down was, as you will see below, after The Great Signboard Robbery and in the 48 hours before polling day, when some very last-minute requests came through.

Putting up the signboards itself requires access to a surprisingly wide-ranging toolkit. I would recommend not trying to whack them into the ground – as we did – with a mallet, but rather getting your hands on a massive sledgehammer. As daunting as it may be for your supporters to watch you walking up their drives with a four-foot weapon, it will save you many hours and much pain. In addition to the hammer, you will need: a staple-gun[53], cable-ties[54], wire-clippers[55], a box or

---

[53] For re-attaching the signboard panels when they fall off from the vibrations of being knocked into the

small stepladder[56], and a van or seriously cavernous estate car. It is worth bearing in mind that putting up boards takes a lot longer than you might expect, especially in a rural area where villages are miles apart. I think we managed to put up between twenty five and thirty a day, with two of us on the job.

The Great Signboard Robbery

Steff and I began to suspect something was up about ten days before polling day. The first sign (excuse the pun) was when we found a broken signboard in a garden in Briston (see picture at the end of the chapter).

The broken board was so neatly stacked that we came to the conclusion it must have been hit

---

ground, or when you rip them off by a misplaced swing with the sledgehammer.

[54] For the households which don't have gardens or have covered over every inch of soil in the gardens with concrete.

[55] For cutting through opposition-supporters' Sky TV Dish cables (a joke, of course), or for cutting off the ends of cable-ties.

[56] If you are short – like me – and cannot reach the top of the signboard.

by passing traffic. The board had been put in at a slight angle in the first instance, making it lean into the road by a few inches) and then piled up for collection by the well-meaning householder.

We took the broken board away, replaced it with a new one (making sure to bang it in as flush to the hedge as possible), and then came back two days later to find that – this time – the board had been removed altogether. Bewilderingly, the household in question belonged to definite supporters that Steff had spoken to on a number of occasions. We worried that perhaps we had done something terrible and mortally offended them. But it turned out that they were as confused as we were.

On the 27 April (according to Whatsapp), I got a message from Steff, who had been out delivering letters in Briston:

"A lot of boards have gone missing! I'm on the phone to the police now."

I replied: "Are you sure people haven't just taken them down?"

"No, it's theft."

"Wow. Jesus," I said.

"I know!"

"Well, aren't we honoured. Must've really

pissed someone off."

We set about calling up every single one of our signboard sites to check whether or not they were missing a board. At the final count, we had over twenty signboards confirmed as missing. Initially, we were outraged, not least because of the time and effort it took to replace the stolen boards. I was close to breaking point: it was just a week until polling day and I was now – like everyone - juggling the county campaign with the deluge of tasks for Norman which had emerged in the wake of the general election announcement.

Time normally reserved for eating and sleeping and, er, my actual day-job, was thin on the ground. We had worked so hard to get those boards in place, and someone had seemingly ripped up a quarter of them without a backward glance. I felt like crying, or hitting someone, or both.

But, in a glorious twist of fate, the whole thing turned out to provide the perfect publicity opportunity. Vengeance is sweet. In fact, by the end of the campaign, we had received so much extra support and media coverage as a result of the theft, that several people accused us of engineering it ourselves.

Having filed an official case with the police, Steff did a short segment for local radio, and the

Eastern Daily Press, our regional newspaper for East Anglia, covered the story with the following article:

"More than 30 poster boards promoting Liberal Democrat candidate Steffan Aquarone in Melton Constable, between Fakenham and Holt, were removed on Thursday and Friday and posters for Conservative candidate Alison Thomas have been taken from Hempnall.

Mr Aquarone said: "Who could it be? A political activist hell-bent on my electoral destruction?

"Perhaps someone who likes our campaign so much they want to plant a whole forest of them in their front garden?"

Mr Aquarone has reported the thefts to Norfolk police and the elections department at North Norfolk District Council.

He said: "We put up 100 posters and I've got an army of volunteers out in cars to check if more are being taken down.

"The council's election office said they have never had something like this happen on this scale so someone has it in for me.

"Someone clearly planned this and it is has the potential to really damage the campaign.

"I don't think any of this is directly

connected my rival candidates as it could be anyone acting on their own.

"This has been reported to the police. It might not seem a big thing to some people but it is theft. Some elderly residents are really quite concerned about people coming to their homes and taking these posters away."

He added: "They've taken the posters with them, so keep an eye out for pathetic-looking bonfires - they really don't burn well."

Anyone with information should contact Norfolk police on 101.[57]

The plot thickened as other pieces of intriguing information come flooding in. For instance, the owner of MossDog sent me an email to say that her partner had heard a car pulling into their driveway around 11pm the previous evening, and that they had come down that morning to find the signboard partially uprooted from the ground.[58]

---

[57] http://www.edp24.co.uk/news/politics/police-investigate-as-norfolk-county-council-election-campaign-posters-for-liberal-democrat-steffan-aquarone-and-conservative-alison-thomas-mysteriously-disappear-1-4994936
[58] Lesson of the day: be sure to hammer signboards into

Around the same time, Steff had a word in the ear of a certain young friend in the community – let's call him Freddy – who is well-connected with North Norfolk's network of more hardcore residents, asking him to keep an eye out. A few days later, Freddy reported back to say that, although he still didn't know whodunnit, he had found a pile of our signboards, broken into pieces and abandoned, in some woods.

To this day, no one has come forward, and no suspects found. But as well as all the extra publicity, people were so outraged on our behalf that many voters got in touch off their own bats, telling us that they had decided to lend Steff their support on polling day. Some even asked for a signboard, specifically because of what had happened (including one person who had previously turned our offer down).

I am not sure what the message at the heart of this story is, except that every cloud has a silver lining. It's also never worth stealing somebody's signs as a political statement. It may be that what doesn't kill candidates only makes them stronger.

---

the ground like there's no tomorrow.

19
The Youth Vote
(Steff)

Immediately after the campaign launch, a very wonderful supporter said she would be interested in donating £500 to the campaign specifically to help encourage younger people to get out and vote. This was an exciting opportunity to carry out some properly tested communications, and we put together a proposal specifically to earn her support as follows:

1. Targeted Facebook ads

To attract the attention of and possible direct means of contact with anyone in the division under the age of 30, we propose running a short burst of paid Facebook video advertising with a tight geographic focus this coming weekend. The concept is to use a meme that has been doing the rounds, where the viewer sees a screen-captured WhatsApp group conversations with various famous people in it discussing a particular issue. In our case it will be fictional politicians, and the call to action will be for people to click through and complete the conversation.

We can target 18-30 year olds with Melton Constable as the epicentre, which will at least mean the leakage due to Facebook's limited geo-targetting would be minimal. This would give us some insight on the key issues as well as contact data and possible voter ID. There would then be a series of follow-up emails principally to communicate the end of the story back to them as well as telling them what happens next and encouraging those who say they are not registered to do so before the Easter deadline.

2. Targeted letters as part of swing/squeeze mailing.

The vast majority of the electors whose dates of birth we know and are under-30 have no canvass data. Therefore, we would propose creating an additional segment for these electors in the swing/squeeze mailing, the main goal of which would be to share the results and highlight specific policy areas within the county manifesto, and therefore Steff's policy agenda, that speak to their interests.

3. Get out the vote.

In polling weeks themselves, we would use a more intensive than usual shorter-form series of email communications, having captured their details, to get out the vote.

In terms of costs, the additional letters @10p each, hand delivered as part of the swing/squeeze delivery, comes to £40 plus £22 for what is typically around 10 per cent of outlying addresses that get Royal Mailed. The video would probably be £80-150. We would propose spending the balance of the budget on Facebook advertising, starting with two small test campaigns to determine the best targeting strategy and the rest would then be spent to drive as many views as possible.

The outcome of this campaign was broadly successful, but no thanks to the Facebook ad spending.

Having run a couple of test campaigns it was clear that the engagement time on the video was not going to lead to many people reaching the call to action at the end, so we revised the purpose of the video simply to attempt to build viewers rather than any other tangible engagement. This certainly mirrored best practice from outside politics: social media, like newspaper and banner advertising, is a way of 'warming up' audiences to a brand or message, not a way of driving direct outcomes or even expressions of interest.

So the video ended up being a nice way of

exploring, with some doubt, whether a man sitting at a desk talking to a camera could satisfy the entertainment preferences of 'Generation Y'.

More encouraging were the effects of the young-person targeting mailing. Given that we were planning on doing a complete targeted swing/squeeze delivered mailing (more on this later) in the closing stages of the campaign, it was relatively easy to include an extra run of letters for named individuals, that would come out of the printer in sequence ready for delivery.

The Lib Dem database system had date of birth details for about a third of electors in Melton Constable, of whom just over 400 were down as aged 30 or under. We obviously don't know how individuals vote but we do know whether they vote, based on the 'marked register' – a copy of the list of names that the people at polling stations put lines through when they have been to vote. At the time of writing, the party has yet to enter the local marked register into Connect, so concluding the effects of this initiative on youth turnout compared to previous years is still 'work in progress'.

But I found a noticeable qualitative difference in the response I had from younger voters in the final days of canvassing. Many of them knew who I was, several of them agreed with the issues I had highlighted, and several of them seemed to have had their minds blown by receiving an actual, physical letter.

20
Polling Week
(Freya)

I just remember polling week as one mad blur. In going back through the master schedule, trying to prompt memories of concrete events, I see that I have inserted the following, increasingly manic instructions:

Monday May 1: delivering and canvassing all day. Take envelopes to Mrs Williams.

Tuesday May 2: Steff to canvass + deliver EDGEFIELD. Freya and Ed to deliver rest of BRISTON + put up extra signboards. All three to canvass and deliver BODHAM.

Wednesday May 3: Steff and Ed to deliver Ryburgh + canvass and deliver LITTLE SNORING Freya and Michael to deliver STIBBARD. Ed to deliver THURSFORD. Michael and Freya to deliver BRININGHAM + MELTON CONSTABLE (or poss Fulmodeston). Steff to canvass and deliver SWANTON NOVERS.

Admittedly I did make separate, slightly more comprehensible schedules for these final days in the run up to eve of polls. Nonetheless, the above does suggest that by Wednesday, I was in no fit state to speak to the public (although, of course, I had to). Steff informs me that, as the week progressed, I developed a universal response to everything from mildly amusing comments through to serious strategy questions, which was simply to laugh hysterically.

I also become increasingly gullible through a combination of lost sleep and information overload, to the extent that Steff managed to convince me that the reason a nearby cherry tree had a perfect square of blossom around its base was not, in fact, because a lawnmower had carved four angles in the grass, but because the tree itself was cuboid.

Don't ask me to explain myself: it was a stressful time.

Miraculously, though, we got through that week without any major crises. This was probably because we were not left to our own devices. Rather, much-needed help arrived in the form of two of Steff's old university friends, Ed and Michael.

We owe a huge amount to Michael and Ed, who carried out the task in hand – putting up with the wrath of an election-weary public and shoving last-minute leaflets through thousands of letterboxes – with a grace and good humour of which surely only saints are capable.

Ed works in theatre production, and set about selling Steff on doorsteps with West-End-stage-worthy zeal. He also had a fairly novel reaction to leafleting. As it turned out, delivering addressed letters inspired obsessive compulsive tendencies in Ed, who literally couldn't bring himself to end the day with any envelopes left in the car. If a house was proving difficult to find, he would simply drive around every random back-road in the vicinity, asking for help from unsuspecting ramblers, until we either found the address or I forced him to let it go.

On Wednesday, we lost Ed for a full hour and a half due to this perfectionism. The plan had been to convene in Ryburgh for a picnic lunch but Ed failed to show up and – because, in much of North Norfolk, you're lucky to get even a smidgen of signal of unless you're in the habit of standing on church-towers – his phone kept going straight to voicemail.

After eating lunch and hanging around for a bit, we decided we had better go in search of him, because anything could have happened: he might have fallen in a ditch, or been eaten by a cow, or been kidnapped by a particularly ardent member of the opposition. We knew roughly where he had been that morning, and in the end we found him in Hempstead, 13 miles away, trying to locate the last four addresses of his delivery round.

Michael, for his part, not only kept all our spirits up with a steady stream of positivity and witticisms, but he also arrived in Norfolk in a vintage Lotus sports car, which introduced an atmosphere of hipster chic hitherto unprecedented in local elections.

The Lotus was an endless source of comedy: I will never forget driving with Michael along a woodland track and then through what felt disconcertingly like a ploughed field, following signs to an elusive 'tower house', the body of the car shaking violently as it negotiated bits of flint, tree stumps, and stray sugar beet.

We did eventually find the tower house, and I was quite sad to find that no one appeared to be home when I popped the letter through the door. I could see no sign of civilisation for miles around, and I wondered what these far-flung tower-dwellers would have made of two strangers showing up on their doorstep in a mud-caked vintage Lotus, raving about the momentous importance of local democracy.

Another amusing feature of the Lotus (which

became less amusing as the hours went by) was that the seats were so low that getting in and out of the car with any semblance of grace required the thigh-power of an Olympic hurdles athlete. On the plus side, by polling day I had achieved more muscle-toning than three years of weekly yoga put together.

Having help during polling week, and especially on polling day itself, makes an inordinate difference. By this late stage in the campaign, as demonstrated earlier, you are likely to have the mental capacity of an amoeba. But what you do during polling week will have a serious impact on the outcome of the election, because it is GOTV time: you have spent six months cultivating a support base and now you need to:

a. Make sure they don't abandon you at the last minute, and
b. Make sure they actually remember to vote

During the last few days of the campaign, be prepared for your opponents to work harder than ever. They will be aiming to systematically undermine, either through voracious charm or direct negative campaigning, all your carefully cultivated messaging about why you are the best thing for community politics since the invention of local taverns. Candidates who have hitherto done and said nothing at all will suddenly hit the campaign trail with the force of an indignant rhinoceros and, without six months of accumulated exhaustion holding them back, they will manage to achieve an annoying amount in a short space of time.[59]

Remember: for many voters, what you present to them in the final few days of the campaign is what is likely to stick out most prominently in their memory, by virtue of being their most recent party-political encounter. I have a friend who once lived in an urban area filled with the politically ambivalent, in which it was not uncommon for families to change their minds about which way they were voting depending on which party had most recently been to visit. He tells me that the signboards displayed along the street at election time changed weekly.

Fortunately, us Norfolkers are a little more

---

[59] Nowhere near enough to win the election, but enough to damage *your* prospects and split the vote. I really haven't the faintest idea what such candidates are motivated by.

averse to change.[60] In my experience, those displaying signboards tend to stick to their guns (and even more voraciously so when they have had their signboard nicked). But unless someone has your name blaring out from their fencepost, they are fully capable of a last-minute change of heart.

In polling week, Michael, Steff, Ed and I focused on two major tasks:

1. Knocking on the doors of our *probs* and *defs* to remind them to vote, in villages which we would not have time to visit on polling day itself, and
2. Delivering the last of the addressed envelopes containing the post-it note with the voting reminder.

---

[60] So would you be if you lived somewhere in which LARGE LORRY NEGOTIATES TIGHT BEND IN NORTH WALSHAM is considered sensational headline news (see: eveningnews24.co.uk, 02 July 2012). You may also be interested to know that our main train service out of the county still has manual doors that require you to stick your arm out of the window to reach the handle (adding, I'm told, fifteen minutes to the Norwich-London journey time). No wonder so few of us venture further south than Thetford.

The door-knocking at this stage was quite different from any other stage in the campaign, because we were actually returning to the doorsteps of people we had *already spoken to* and could say with some confidence were our supporters. As per the GOTV gospel, the single most important thing in polling week is to get those most likely to vote for you to turn up to the polling station on Thursday.

The time for reaching and convincing brand new people or talking to the thoroughly unsure is over. The one exception to this is squeeze voters: because our data was suggesting it was going to be a seriously close call between us and the Conservatives, we did keep knocking on the doors of soft Labour voters and Red Lib Dems right up until the day before polling day.

Our message was simple: this late on, the data is pretty robust, and it is telling us in no uncertain terms that Labour cannot win. On the other hand, the Tories have a very good chance of winning, and none of us want that. So please will you 'lend us' your vote on Thursday, to keep out the Blues?

Our experience on the doorstep with these voters was fairly promising: people who had wanted to make a statement about their loyalty to the Red camp earlier on in the year were more willing, this late in the game, to make tactical decisions, especially with the threat of a Tory win so real and imminent.

As I mentioned earlier, we did not deliver Eve of Polls leaflets, because we were running behind on our envelope delivery. Instead, we hoped that our final envelope – particularly because it was personally addressed to our supporter base – might achieve the same goal of reminding people about the election.

I made sure that the bulk of the delivery fell on the shoulders of Michael, Ed and me, so that Steff could spend almost all of that final week on doors. We also did all we could to maximise our visibility in the community: each day in polling week, we popped into at least one of the division's many fine pubs.

It was during one of these pit-stops that Steff ended up chatting to a bloke at the bar who, as it turned out, lived in one of the closes where a number of our signboards had been stolen. He had heard all about the saga and the two of them got chatting. By the end of the conversation, they were shaking hands and Steff was promising to put up a board in the man's front garden that afternoon!

Steff became such a familiar face at Briston's Three Horseshoes over the course of the campaign that, when he went in for a pint the day after the count, the place erupted in cheers. Truly, there are few things that made it all feel as worth it.

21
Polling day
(Freya)

Polling day itself began with a text message at 5.42am from our sister, Beth, who lives in Kenya (and is therefore three hours ahead). She said: "Last night I dreamt I tamed an eagle owl to be part of your campaign. You can thank me later."

A good omen, surely.

Polling day is weird because it's a little like waking up on the morning of a high-stakes exam, but one for which most of the outcome is already decided. Unlike with exams, where it is possible to do masses of preparation in the run up and have it all obliterated by sheer bad luck on the day by a rubbish question, unfortunate cycling incident or fear-induced memory loss – a candidate would have to do something seriously ridiculous on polling day to undo the previous six months' work.

So you at least get to start the day in the comforting knowledge that the outcome is 90 per cent in the lap of the gods. Of course, that remaining ten per cent can probably swing the entire outcome, so don't just write the day off and crawl back under your duvet, or you might find that – despite that week's work – half of your support base still forgets there's an election on.[61]

In reality, no amount of rationalising about how much work you have done can really assuage the pain of waking up at 4.30am, or make the sugar-and-caffeine-fuelled whirlwind of the eighteen hours to come any less panic-stricken.

Michael, Steff and I piled into the car at about 5.30am and set off for Saxthorpe and Corpusty, two idyllic villages separated by a river at the edge of the division.[62] We started delivering Good Morning leaflets around 6.15, and didn't stop until over three and a half hours later, when we collapsed into the chairs outside Ryburgh village shop, desperately reaching for the plunger on the cafetiere.

I remember remarking jovially at this point

---

[61] I'm always slightly horrified by how many people swear they have no idea that it is polling day. It just goes to show, as we argued earlier, that you aren't doing 'too much' campaigning until everybody is thoroughly sick of your face, and chanting "Thursday May 4, Thursday May 4" in their sleep.

[62] Ed had limited time off work, and had returned to London on Wednesday evening.

that there were only twelve hours to go until close of polls. The comment elicited quite a barrage of abuse from Steff and Michael.

After re-fuelling on caffeine, we set off for Briston and Melton Constable, where we were to spend the rest of the day.[63] Door-knocking on polling day is oriented around one simple question: has that person been out to vote today? If the answer is yes, ask them which way they voted, thank them, and retreat swiftly. If the answer is no, impress upon them how earth-shatteringly vital it is that they go and do so, and say that the data is showing you might lose by as few as a handful of votes.[64]

Regardless of the actual outcome, there will be

---

[63] Briston is the biggest village in the division by far, containing around a third of the division's registered voters, and is located right beside Melton Constable, the smaller village after which the division is named.
[64] Unless this is a total lie and you are either clearly going to win by a landslide, or be totally slaughtered. Your data is unlikely to be to so clear-cut either way, but obviously tailor your message as appropriate: for example, there is a chance we might win here for the first time in fifteen years, or it's looking very promising but we really can't be sure, and so on.

at least one point in the day where you are wildly optimistic about your chances, and another where you are totally convinced you have lost. Your capacity for rational thought is so decimated by this stage, that you need only speak to two impassioned Green voters who you had down on your records as Liberals to conclude that there has been a massive, unprecedented swing to the Green Party and that you are going to lose to them by hundreds of votes.

This emotional rollercoaster is par for the course and the best thing, if you can, is to ignore your addled inner monologue and plug on till close of polls.

We door-knocked for a couple of hours and then paused for a quick lunch on a park bench beside the main road. This was quite a central location, close to Astley Primary, the school with which Steff had built a relationship through the Lollipop Lady campaign. During our lunch, I remember at least a dozen people stopping to chat and wish us luck.

A lady who we had met on quite a few occasions also stopped by with her two dogs – who were wearing tiny coats – and asked if she could have a couple of our Lib Dem badges to pin on to them.

Other bizarre highlights of the day included

discovering that one supporter had sellotaped a picture of Steff's face (from the front of one of our leaflets) to their recycling bin and being given a free copy of someone's memoirs on the doorstep (see picture at the end of the chapter).

Astonishingly, we only crossed over with our opponents once, when the UKIP candidate drove through the middle of the village with a tannoy, shouting: 'Good people of Melton Constable, vote UKIP today!'

There are some times on polling day which are more 'golden' than others in terms of opportunities for catching people and reminding them to vote. Because the vast majority of people will be out at work on a Thursday, these times are the eerie hours of dawn in which you plaster people's doormats with Good Morning leaflets before they set off to work, and then 5-9pm, when people come home from work.

So it is important to pace yourself to make sure you are not too exhausted by early evening to go full throttle for that crucial 5-9pm time-slot.

So, after lunch, we carried on door-knocking until 4pm, at which point we retreated for an hour to a pre-planned 'safe house' in order to gear up for the final push. This house belonged to our friend and fellow campaigner Roberta's son and daughter-in-law, who very generously allowed us to use their conservatory as a base for the afternoon and evening. When the three of us arrived, somewhat the worse for wear, Roberta immediately made masses of tea and coffee and presented us with a tin full of homemade baking. I can honestly say I have never been more overjoyed by the sight of a flapjack than I was that grey polling day afternoon.

On polling day for general elections, or for local elections in more densely populated areas, the campaigns team will usually set up a *Committee Room* in a central location. The committee room acts as the beating heart of polling day operations. It provides you with space methodically to scatter your myriad bits of important paper (canvassing sheets, delivery maps, random notes like 'Mrs Tibbs needs a lift to the polling station at 1.15 *precisely* or she'll miss the cricket'), a source of electricity and wifi, and a steady supply of caffeinated drinks.

If you are running a very complex polling day, having a committee room is vital. For Norman Lamb's general election campaign, we had about 200 volunteers out, and ran three committee rooms in strategic locations across the constituency. We were able to advertise the whereabouts of the committee rooms to our volunteer network and then people could show up at their preferred location at any time of day, collect a delivery bundle or a canvassing pack, and set off to pound the streets.

If you are in charge of a committee room, then there are a few things to bear in mind:

- As well as all the campaigning essentials, make sure you have masses of clipboards, pens and paper, hot drinks, milk and snacks.
- Somebody permanently based at the committee room needs to be fully familiar with Connect and its frustrating idiosyncrasies, so that they can process the telling and door-knocking data, print new canvass sheets, field phone banking queries, and not panic too much when the whole thing crashes.
- Unless all your volunteers as using Minivan, you must have access to a printer: the door-knocking lists will shrink as the day goes by and the telling and door-knocking data is processed, so you need to be able to print new sheets on demand. It is best, if possible, to use a laser printer, because if it rains, the last thing you want to be dealing with is canvassing sheets covered in illegible smudges.
- There are laws regarding committee rooms. It is, for instance, illegal to 'treat' voters with "meat, drink or entertainment or provision" in the hope

that they will vote for you or refrain from voting, so make sure you don't go handing out sweets on doorsteps. It is a legal requirement that you clearly advertise your committee room with a sign placed on an externally-facing window or wall.

You must also display the full list of committee room-related laws somewhere where your volunteers can see it. This list can be accessed online, or you can ask your local party if they own a hard copy. Do check in with your election agent about legal requirements, as what is and isn't necessary changes periodically, and they will able to fill you in.

Steff and I did not run a committee room for the whole of polling day. This was partly because the division is so disparately populated and partly because, as is usually the case with local elections, there were so few of us actually out campaigning; we could basically all fit into one roaming committee room in the form of Steff's car.

But we did anticipate that we would be in need of a committee room by late afternoon, not only as somewhere to flop on a sofa for an hour and recuperate, but also because, by that time, we had door-knocked almost all of the key streets in Briston and Melton Constable, and I needed to log in to Connect to update the lists for Minivan.

Even more importantly, some of our friends living outside Norfolk – Calum and Emily – had responded to our online pleas and agreed to do some phone-banking. The great thing about phone-banking is that it can be done from anywhere, and it is theoretically simple to set up. But you do need access to the internet and if your laptop is anything like mine, its battery life leaves much to be desired, so a plug socket also comes in handy.

While we all had our fourth coffee of the day, I beavered away at Connect while Michael folded more doorstep leaflets and Steff updated his Facebook and Twitter with polling day reminders. It was around this time that fresh blood arrived in the form of Steff's childhood friend, Aaron. When there are so few hands on deck, an additional pair makes a huge difference, especially in those crucial last hours of the day.

I sent Michael, Steff and Aaron back off into the Briston wilderness and set about trying to get my head around Connect's phone bank software for Calum and Emily.

The following hour turned out to be by far the most stressful of the day. When I said that phone banking is theoretically simple, I really did mean theoretically. There are, confusingly, two ways to log into Connect: one using a 'VAN ID' and one using a 'Connect log in'. The latter requires a proper Connect account, set up by someone with 'administrator' status and allows you access to most of Connect's data and functions. The former, however, can be created by anyone and just allows them access to Minivan and the 'virtual phone bank', from which they can then download fixed lists made by someone with full access.

With me so far? Well, I have a proper Connect log in, and had made all the lists ready for Calum and Emily to hit the phones. But for some bizarre reason which I am yet to fully understand, Connect first refused to recognise their VAN IDs at the log-in stage and then, when that problem miraculously resolved itself, refused to give them access to the lists I had created.

Because of the terrible phone reception, I had sit outside in the open boot of Steff's car, my laptop balanced on my knee, giving Calum and Emily desperate instructions over a crackling phone line for increasingly unlikely solutions to the problem. I was aware with every passing minute that opportunities to reach voters were slipping sickeningly away from us.

Eventually, we did resolve the problem, and Emily and Calum were able to make their calls, though I honestly cannot remember how we managed it. Key lesson: it is probably best to do a test-run of your phone-banking *before* the big day, and make sure you know how to troubleshoot common problems because, however much I like to blame Connect for that particular crisis, it was probably more due to my ignorance of the software.

At about 8.30pm, Steff, Michael, Aaron and I piled into the car and headed back to my parents' house in Blickling, about 25 minutes down the road, where we made enormous gin and tonics and, for one final hour, hit the phones. Anyone walking into the house during that time would have seen a very odd sight: people hunched at the top of the stairs, in the corners of first floor bedrooms, by the kitchen window – all the places where it is possible to get a shred of mobile signal (only one of us, of course, could use the landline), precariously balancing massive glasses of gin on windowsills and chairs, and talking at 100 mph to random members of the public.

And then it was all over. It is an oddly underwhelming moment when you reach 10 o'clock and know that the polls have closed. What with all the build up, you sort of expect a brass band to turn up and erupt into fanfare. Instead, we all convened in the kitchen from our various corners of the house, and just burst out laughing.

It took about two hours for the adrenaline to

drain away. I finally got into the bath close to midnight, and realised with a shock that I had forgotten to eat any proper food since lunchtime, 11 hours previously. But at least I fell asleep that night thinking, well, we gave it our best shot. Now it really was in the lap of the gods.

22

The count

(Steff)

'The count' is what happens after the polling stations have closed and it is time for people who normally work for the council by day to pull an all-nighter going through all the bits of paper to work out who has won.

As ways of building anticipation ahead of announcing results go, political counts are about as far removed from the Oscars as it is possible to be – although you wouldn't know this from the clamouring excitement and competitiveness for tickets (which are strictly limited).

For some people, the count is the highlight of their social calendar: they shower, get dressed up and sneak in illicit alcohol. But not at ours: in what was a welcome relief, the Norfolk County Council election count for 2017 took place the following day (apparently this saves money), although it was hard to tell whether it was dark or light outside from the confines of North Walsham High School sports hall.

Going to the count when you are not actually

counting anything has several useful purposes, for example: you get to 'sample' the ballot boxes as they are tipped out and counted. This gives you an indication of where your votes came from and where, to the nearest village, your actual support is highest.

I had a very good feeling about two parts of the campaign: postal votes, and Briston. Based on other divisions, we started to see that postal votes were generally more in our favour. And in Briston the lollipop lady campaign had been a big issue even though most of the users were in neighbouring Melton Constable, and it represented a full quarter of the division in population terms. It was also the village we had visited the most, and where we'd had lots of lovely feedback on polling day itself.

All the votes from Briston were in two boxes. As luck would have it, the postal vote and Briston boxes were the very last three to be opened. I am pleased with my majority of 420 but, up until that point, the turnout from the last three boxes could have swung it either way. The sample tally I saw was off the scale – ridiculously disproportionate compared to the actual result for Briston, which was still very favourable. But I knew at that point we had probably done it.

Thank you, again, Briston.

At the count, you also get to check that the people counting are not part of a conspiracy to undermine representative democracy, one local election at a time. And, more importantly, you get to fraternise with your opponents.

Yes: after fighting each other ceaselessly for months, you and your chosen lucky friends or family members can now stand shoulder-to-shoulder with your opponents with clipboards while the outcomes of your efforts are laid bare – tortuously slowly.

And it really is tortuous, because that is just the start. At this stage, the ballot papers have just been counted to make sure their number matches the number of people the polling station recorded as having voted. Then they get put into piles, and those piles get counted, and you find yourself doubting whether you were even on some of the ballot papers, let alone stand a chance of winning.

At general election counts, there is often someone with a laptop, crunching the sampling as it comes in, who can usually give a pretty good indication of the outcome once the ballot papers have all been counted. But at local elections, there is so much going on, and not enough sampling, to really get a clear picture, although you can obviously start to tell which villages really hated you.

To add to all this, the lovely people who you have campaigned alongside are going through the same thing at inevitably different speeds, which makes the count somewhere between the Worst Oscars Ever and A-level results day. They even have media there to get pictures of people when it is all over.

Let me briefly say that not all my competitors stayed for the whole thing. The one who left first refused to shake my hand. But another of my erstwhile opponents stayed to the end, and actually had the grace to call it in my favour when all the papers were being put into piles. I was nowhere near that confident by that stage, so hearing that really made me think we might have done it.

But that wasn't the end because the Norfolk Conservative party insisted the result wasn't declared until a discrepancy of nine was resolved. The returning officer had a clear majority of more than 400, but there were nine ballot papers too many. So we had to do a recount. This meant we were the last division to announce (they start to emerge in dribs and drabs after a few hours) and that there was nobody else in the sports hall apart from us, a few Conservatives, the returning officer and the media.

In public-to-press ratio terms, it must have

been at the extreme end of things. But some of our lovely colleagues stuck around – including Sarah Tustin, Ed Maxfield, and Pierre and Sarah Bütikofer – right until the end.[65] And although we knew we had won, we had to look surprised and delighted – which paid off, because the clip of us winning was the one that made it onto BBC Look East that evening.

And then I was a councillor.

How incredibly surreal.

And brilliant!

---

[65] Sarah is one of the toughest fighters I have come across in politics so far. She narrowly missed out winning her division in 2013, despite Freya's help and worked tirelessly for four years to bring home the bacon in 2017 in a highly unpredictable area where the UKIP incumbent had run half the town, which itself was traditionally Conservative. Freya and I were nearly as pleased with Sarah's victory as we were with ours.

23

The thank you party

(Freya)

Saying thank you to your volunteers matters. From a really cynical, exploitative perspective, it makes them more likely to help you or other candidates in the future. But more importantly, from a human perspective, these are people who have given up their precious free time simply to promote your chances of political success, and they deserve to be recognised.

For sure, many of us willingly help candidates because we believe that they will make politics better in some way, that they are good people who have the potential to make a difference. But nonetheless, and especially if you lose the election, volunteering for political campaigns is something of a thankless task.

Steff and I did a couple of things throughout the campaign to try and express to our volunteers how grateful we were for their tolerance and travail. Earlier on, in the chapter about volunteers, I mentioned trying to check in regularly with our deliverers, to make sure they were not suffering in silence, and to build genuine relationships. And in Steff's chapter on fund-raising, he talked about rewarding donors, who might not be able to make it along to a thank you party.

There are other, simple things you can do to make people feel valued. When Steff and I went away for a weekend in the last month of the campaign, to attend our party conference in York, we sent postcards to every person who had helped us so far – in whatever way, big or small – just saying we appreciated it and noting that the end was in sight.[66]

---

[66] At the time, so close to polling day, we were quite worried about taking this time off and even jokingly accused by Norman Lamb of 'skiving'! But we went with the sole purpose of learning from the conference training programme. Party conference offers a series of workshops and seminars – many of them run by ALDC – on everything from detailed explanations of how to analyse canvass data to 'door knocking for beginners'. Though the sessions did vary in quality, overall we decided that going had been well worth the time and money, and we gleaned lots of tips for the campaign. There are also other useful resources at conference, such as the Ask An Expert stand in the exhibition hall,

We also threw a thank you party. I am really not sure to this day when I found the time to organise it in those frantic weeks before polling day, but it definitely happened – albeit in a slightly slapdash kind of way. In true local politics style, we held the party in one of the division's many village halls. The village hall also, fittingly, had no phone reception and no wifi.

About a fortnight before polling day, I rang up the head of the village hall committee and spoke to someone who I am not sure was overly keen on the idea of a party political piss-up happening on their premises, especially once they realised they was talking to a young – and therefore especially untrustworthy – Liberal Democrat. I had to reassure them that many of the party guests would be well past retirement age and that although, in my experience of Norfolk, age is no indicator whatsoever of capacity for unruly

where you can take all your niche Connect questions to a long-suffering software representative. Finally, the experience of being surrounded by hundreds of other Lib Dems, all fighting for the same cause across the country and experiencing - if not the same then similar - frustrations and roadblocks, was just really heartening.

behaviour, she would at least not be dealing with a load of drunken adolescents.

I was also careful to explain that the party would go ahead regardless of the outcome of the election, and that it was therefore not about making a party-political statement but simply about thanking people for all their support. It did also help that some family friends of ours – who were also invited to the party – were fellow members of the committee and would be invited too.[67]

We held the party the Saturday after polling day and invited every single person we could think of who had anything to do with the campaign: deliverers, envelope-addressers, door-knockers, phone-bankers, donors, people from the local party office, as well as a handful of other county candidates from North Norfolk and Broadland.

Fortunately, the village hall had its own well-stocked cash bar, so we paid for everyone to have one drink for free, and then asked them to bring a handful of coins for the rest. I went to a

---

[67] Partly for tolerating us showing up unexpectedly on their doorstep demanding cups of tea every time we happened to be door-knocking or leafleting in the village.

supermarket earlier in the day, got a bit excited in the post-count euphoria, and bought half the available stock of quiches and party rings.

Finally, we hooked up a microphone to a speaker, so that Steff and I could say a few words. And Norman too, who we allowed some limelight to try and convince our exhausted volunteers to help with the general election which was just three weeks away.

Well over fifty people came to the party, some from as far as the distant lands of Norwich. Elections can be truly anticlimactic, even if the outcome is in your favour. Because, unless you are the winning candidate, without everyone getting together to mark the occasion you just finish up your last delivery round, smile (or groan) at the result the next day, and then go back to whatever life you were leading before your evenings became punctuated by endless bloody leafleting.

Without the opportunity to come together, many of those involved in your campaign may never meet, because one of the brilliant things about political campaigns is that they draw on people from so many different walks of life. So I think it is really important that we all descended on a village hall to celebrate.

It was also good to see so many of the wonderful people we had met during the campaign gathered in one place, and it gave us the perfect chance to thank everyone in what is surely the only proper way: with food and alcohol.

But, most importantly, the party rounded off the whole reckless, ridiculous adventure: it allowed us all to sit back in a chair, raise a glass, and say *we did it*.

24
Epilogue

While we were proof reading the book, Freya explained that a lot of undergraduates with long reading lists often don't have time to read the 'middle', meaning the introduction and conclusion chapters are the most important. So we went through all the things we thought we'd learned and summarised them as follows. A lot of the old rules are valid, like:

- Start early and work hard
- Totally ignore your opponents
- Put effort into volunteer recruitment and management
- Focus campaign activity using data
- Get involved with local issues campaigns

But we also did a number of things that went against the received wisdom:

We didn't shy away from national issues, values or political platforms. In fact we spoke strongly and proudly about liberal values, and politely disagreed with people without reservation.

Our literature was subject to a design refresh that was drawn from the same brief as our messaging so that form matched content.

We didn't focus much time at all on social media.

We got press coverage by making things happen and then writing about the news, rather than trying to score party political points in letters pages.

And we did several things that are almost certainly part and parcel of how elections have long been fought, but which don't seem to get said loudly enough:

- We made ourselves useful rather than just talking about stuff.
- We got to grips with Connect ourselves.
- We had someone (Freya) who was with the candidate (Steff) throughout the campaign to run things.
- We made use of digital tools like a shared online master plan, diaries, casework management and Minivan.
- We raised some proper money although had to top it up with personal funds.

And above all: we had a clear purpose and could

pitch it with conviction and authenticity. This is surely the fuel that makes everything else happen.

**

I would like to thank a lot of people for helping make this campaign a success: from the people who I met once on a training course who decided to donate to my crowdfunding, to the family and friends of old who stepped up and got involved and of course local party colleagues and fellow candidates. And especially to the people I didn't know at all until it all started, who gave so freely of their time because they decided I was worth supporting and wanted to get me elected.

So much of this campaign has been down to Freya. She is a truly remarkable person: the smartest I have ever encountered, and in a disgusting number of ways. I was unbelievably lucky to have her as my campaign manager, so far beyond her pay grade. It is a bit like if Elton John played at your wedding because he was mates with you at school.

Freya has the fortitude of an ox and a near-fanatical belligerence that gets things done. She is also frustratingly honest, ethical and kind. The short answer to "how we won a local election in six months" is "by putting Freya in charge". If she doesn't go for it herself, I'm sure she will be king or queen-maker to a prime minister some day.

So there is the lesson: go and find a Freya. There are more people like her out there. And you might not even need to work *quite* as hard as we did. But I hope that, in sharing our experiences of this campaign, you will find you can do it too.

But before you jump into it, think carefully about whether you're prepared to put in what it takes. Is your frustration at some sort of injustice strong enough for you to want to do everything to win? Because if not, then go and help someone else who is instead, and you will still have earned that great feeling of achievement when they get in.

Don't stand as a half-hearted gesture, because it means your politics will be half-hearted. There are lots of people who really believe in us, and lots more of them would vote for us if we actually stated behaving like we intended to win, and that means focusing our efforts where we will.

There are of course people who vote for us even though we stand no chance. Like the woman in Little Bodham who was at the end of a row of houses, half of which were brandishing UKIP posters. "You're our only hope!" she shouted out of her window, after I had just posted something through her letterbox. It made me cry.

Don't insult these people, whose values mean

we are the only party they can support, despite our imperfections, and who are isolated in a sea of projection, bigotry and hopelessness: stand if you mean to fight, and intend to win.

Finally, here are two of my favourite things that people in my division wrote (the first was not an elector, because they were a child):

"Vote Liberal Democrats – they give money to the poor."

"You've been all over North Norfolk like a rash. We still expect to see a presence once all the self congratulatory back-slapping has finished."

-THINGS-
i have
DONE
Since I started campaigning
in December

[faded text]

Mal Edgefield

• Supported the parents of Astley School to save their lollipop lady

• Worked with Norman Lamb to survey more than 1,500 people in the community about their experiences of the health service

• Begun exploring a radical way of improving rural mobile phone and broadband coverage involving more than 100 people so far

• Carried out the biggest ever consultation on bus services in the area

• Dealt with more than 50 individual pieces of case work for local residents

• Supported three families with highly complex mental health, disability and employment rights issues

• Reported numerous potholes, many of which have already been fixed

[faded text]

Norman Lamb, MP for
North Norfolk

-THINGS-
i will
DO
If I win on May 4th

• Campaign to integrate health and social care services in Norfolk - help me get started by putting up the enclosed poster in your window!

• Put pressure on Clinical Commissioning Groups to commit a larger proportion of their resources to mental health services

• Keep Children's Centres open and continue to support mobile libraries

• Promote the county policy of recovering the cost of repairing road damage caused by large vehicles

• Promote super centres for the collection of extended ranges of recyclable materials

[faded text]

Emma, Wood Norton

• Help set up community speed watch teams in every village and campaign for the most effective measures to be put in place based on national evidence

• Ensure official bodies with responsibility for flooding work together on long-term management strategies especially for drainage and surface water systems

• Pursue the target of broadband and indoor mobile phone signal for 100% of Norfolk properties by March 2020

• Continue the long-held liberal policy of supporting restorative justice - proven to reduce offending and repair damage caused to victims, families and communities

• Hold weekly surgeries both in person and on social media

Vote for
Steffan AQUARONE [X]
on May 4th

Melton Constable

FOCUS

WE DID IT
MORE IMPORTANTLY,
YOU DID IT

38 lollipop ladies across Norfolk have been saved thanks to a successful campaign led by the people of Briston and Melton Constable, helped by Liberal Democrat candidate Steffan Aquarone.

The County Council's decision to halt their removal came after campaigners delivered a petition signed by over 500 people in connection with Astley Primary School alone!

Steff worked over Christmas with local parent Karen Cornish on an eight-page submission outlining how the Council had got the numbers wrong and that the crossing at Astley Primary School should be saved - even according to their own guidelines. He helped organise the protest outside County Hall on the morning of the meeting that would decide the lollipop ladies' fate, which received widespread media coverage.

"It was very much a team effort but we had very valuable support and direction from Steff" said Karen. "It's reassuring to know that the children of Astley Primary will continue to be protected by our most excellent lollipop lady."

"This is about a local community getting together to make things happen, and constructively challenge the authorities that have so much influence over our lives" Steff said.

"It's not about budgets, it's about putting children first, which I think has now been done."

MOBILE PHONE SIGNAL IN NORFOLK

Lots of people in North Norfolk suffer from poor or non-existent phone coverage, and it affects people from all walks of life.

It's clear neither the Government nor the big mobile phone companies are going to invest the time and money that's needed to roll out proper phone and data coverage across the constituency.

But there is another way...

We've looked at all the options and decided it's time to take matters into our own hands. Later this year we're going to set up community-owned mobile phone company that will plug the gaps and bring coverage to the hardest to reach areas.

And we need your help to do it!

Steffan Aquarone and Norman Lamb MP will be joined by mobile industry experts on 10th February in Cromer to share more about the project and how you can get involved.
Contact Steff (overleaf) for more details about the time and place.

Other HOW TO books from the Real Press

How to become a freelance writer

This is a manual about freelance writing with a difference. It won't tell you how to write or what to write. It assumes you know these things already. It doesn't set out to equip you for a brief period of freelancing.

It will, on the other hand, tell you how to go about living a writer's life in a practical way – how to plan ahead, how to shape your career, how to find clients and how to deal with the money. It will tell you how to make a life out of writing without falling into the many little traps that are set for us once we embark on the idea.

If you are thinking of changing your life, you may be tempted to buy many other books about how to write, or taking the first technical steps into becoming a freelancer – but this book will set you on the path to live that life.

www.therealpress.co.uk